Lord Make It Plain

So I Can Understand

Definitions of Common Christian Words

By
James Edward

Copyright © 2016 James Edward

All rights reserved.

Title ID: 5705247

ISBN-13: 978-1517095987

For more Information Contact:
James Edward
Lord Make It Plain
P.O. Box 7643
Greensboro, N.C. 27417

Email: James@LordMakeItPlain.com
www.LordMakeItPlain.com

James Edward

INTRODUCTION

Why did I write this book? I began this labor of love over twenty two years ago when I accepted Jesus. I did not grow up going to church so when I came in I noticed a lot of words and phrases that I had never heard of before and so I didn't know what they meant.

I would have to go to the dictionary and look them up and then I would look up scriptures where the words were used to get a better understanding of what the author was saying.

For instance my first Bible was the King James Version and in 1 Corinthians 13:4 it says *"Charity suffereth long, and is kind; charity envieth not; charity vaunteth not itself, is not puffed up,"*

Ok...I was really lost on that one because we don't use those words anymore or at least not in the same context because meanings change. So I had to look up charity for instance and I saw that that word is just love, so therefore "love suffereth long". I could pretty much make out what suffereth means even though we don't speak 16th century English.

Another one that got me was meek as used in *Matthew 11:29 Take my yoke upon you, and learn of me; for I am meek and lowly in heart: and ye shall find rest unto your souls.*
Well upon looking that word up I discovered that meek actually means "power under control" meaning someone has the ability or right to use power, but they refrain from it namely for the other persons sake. Understanding that opens up that scripture quite a bit for me and especially *Numbers 12:3 Now the man Moses was very meek, above all the men which were upon the face of the earth.*
I always thought it was saying Moses was weak because for us today we associate meek with weak, but meek is almost the exact opposite of

weak. Picture a parent who allows a child to express himself or an employer who knows they have the authority and ability to tell the employee to do something because they are the boss, but instead they allow the employee to contribute their opinion for consideration.

Moses and Jesus weren't weak; they were tolerant of the others for compassions sake if you will.

Another word I had to look up was minister because I wanted to know what it meant when the scripture says the angels came to minister to Jesus in *Matthew 4:11*. Minister means to help. Very simple so a Minister is one who helps.

So now when we read *Hebrews 1:14 about the purpose of Angels and it says "Are they not all ministering spirits, sent forth to minister for them who shall be heirs of salvation?"*

Now I can understand that they are helping spirits sent to help those that are the heirs of salvation (me and you if you are a saint).

Again even the word Saint confused me because I thought saints were in Heaven, but then I learned that saint just means a Christian believer. In almost all of Paul's letters he refers to the Saint's here and there and such. So I found out that I am a Saint...Saint James – hmmm.

My prayer early on was to understand the scriptures because *Proverbs 4:7 says "Wisdom is the principal thing; Therefore get wisdom. And in all your getting, get understanding."*

So that's where the name of this book came from "Lord Make It Plain – So I Can Understand". To me my life depends on getting this thing so I needed to get it in the simplest manner possible.

So Saint James (I can hear you now)...why all the Greek?

Well that's a good question and another one I had to learn about. Here is a great revelation for some. Your Bible was not written in English and Jesus did not speak English. He actually spoke Hebrew and Aramaic and it's very likely He knew Greek because since after Alexander the Great conquered Jerusalem Greek became the language of government and business.

Hebrew would have been used in schools, the Temple and "proper" settings, but since He and His disciples were from Nazareth which was part of the Judean region they would have spoken Aramaic which was the most common language in that area.

The Old Testament was written in Hebrew and the New Testament was written in Greek. In my research I couldn't find conclusively that Jesus spoke Greek, but since we know His disciples did then I would tend to believe Jesus did also.

In 1604 King James began the task of translating the Bible into what was for him modern day English and it was completed in 1611. So this version is one thousand five hundred and thirty eight years after Jesus' ascension.

I appreciate the King James Version, but I don't speak that language so early on it frustrated me. Well meaning friends would tell me to pray for understanding of it. My prayers led me to reading the New King James and New International Versions. For me the desire to understand is too strong.

So again why Greek?

Greek is the language of the New Testament and unfortunately the translators didn't always do the best job of conveying the meanings from one language to another.

Greek is much, much more descriptive than English. The perfect example of this is the word love. The Greeks had several words to describe depending on the relationship such as the love for your children is different than the love you feel for your wife or a brother or even the love you feel for the world whereas in English have only one.

Agape love which is the love of God as described in 1 Corinthians 13.

There is also phileo or brotherly love as translated in *1 Samuel 18:1-2 As soon as he had finished speaking to Saul, the soul of Jonathan was knit to the soul of David, and Jonathan loved him as his own soul.*

The Greeks also used eros or erotic love to describe the love between a husband and wife. The Song of Solomon is written entirely from this perspective even though it was written in Hebrew.

In Colossians 3:5 Paul tells us to flee sexual immorality which is basically eros love perverted.

Then there is also Ludus or playful love such as children have. Pragma which describes the deep understanding which comes from long term marriage.

So you can see why when you want a clearer understanding it's important to delve deeper. This takes nothing away from the word of God being infallible, but we have to remember that although it is, men aren't and when we translate with the best intentions we sometimes make mistakes.

Hope is another word I like. In English if you say you are hoping for something you mean it's fifty, fifty and you might get it or you might not. Not so for Bible hope. In the Greek the word used was for hope is elpis which means a joyful, confident expectation of good. This is not maybe so, maybe no. This is definite. The thing being hoped for is definitely coming.

Think about it like this...it's two days before Christmas and you know your parents got you something good, but you can't open it until

Christmas. You *know* it's coming and you're excitedly anticipating it, not wondering if you'll get it or not.

This is what was meant when Paul writes in *2 Corinthians 1:7 And our hope for you [our confident expectation of good for you] is firmly grounded [assured and unshaken], since we know that just as you share as partners in our sufferings, so also you share as partners in our comfort.*

Or in Hebrews 1:1 when the writer says "*Now faith is the assurance of things hoped for, the evidence of things not seen.*"

In this case that hope in the promise and who promised it is just as good as the thing itself and they were just waiting for the thing to come.

Although I started this book over twenty years ago I did not know enough to finish it then (and I may not even know enough now), but I have learned a lot and the more I learn the more I know I'm missing something – ugh!

I'm writing this to pass on what I do know to help (minister to) someone else on their trip, I'm sharing it in the hope (joyful, confident expectation of good) that it will bless someone else to get an understanding also.

James

James Edward

CONTENTS

INTRODUCTION 4

ABUNDANT 21

ACKNOWLEDGE 21

ADAM 22

ADULTERY 23

ANGELS 23

AMEN 24

ANOINT 24

APOSTLE 25

ASK 25

AUTHORITY 26

BAPTISM 27

BELIEVE 27

BIBLE 28

BISHOP (Overseer) 29

BLASPHEME 30

BLESS 31

James Edward

BLESSED	31
CAPTIVE	33
CARE	33
CAREFUL	33
CARES	34
CHEERFUL	34
CHEATING	35
CHRIST/MESSIAH (Anointed)	35
CHURCH (called ones)	36
COMFORT/COMFORTER	36
COMPASSION	37
CONDEMN	38
CONFESS	38
CONGREGATION	39
CONFORM	39
CONFIDENCE	40
CONVOCATION	40
CONVOKING	40
CONSECRATE	41

COUNSELOR/COUNSEL 41

COVENANT 42

CREATOR 43

CREATE 43

CULT 44

CURSE 44

DEACON 47

DEMON 47

DENY 48

DESIRE 48

DOMINION 48

DOUBT 49

EARNEST 51

ELOHIM 51

ENEMY 52

ENVY 53

ETERNAL LIFE 53

ETERNITY/ETERNAL 54

EVANGELIST 54

James Edward

EVIL	55
FAIR	57
FAITH	57
FALLEN FROM GRACE	60
FATHER	61
FAVOR	62
FEAR	62
FELLOWSHIP	63
FOOL	64
FORNICATION	64
FORGIVE	64
FORSAKEN	65
FREE	65
GENEROUS	67
GENTILE	67
GENTLE	68
GLAD	68
GLORY	68
GOD	69

GOOD	70
GOSPEL (Almost too good to be true news)	70
GOSSIP	71
GRACE (Do give me what I don't deserve)	72
GUILTY	72
GREED	73
HAPPY/HAPPINESS	75
HEAL	75
HEALTH	75
HEIR	76
HELL	76
HELP	76
HIGH PRIEST	77
HOLIDAY (holy day)	77
HOLY (set apart for God)	78
HOLY SPIRIT	79
HOMOSEXUAL	79
HONEST	80
HOPE	80

James Edward

IMAGE (see likeness also) 83

INIQUITY 83

INVISIBLE 84

JEALOUSY 87

JEW 88

JOY 88

JUSTICE 89

JUSTIFICATION 89

JUSTIFY/JUSTIFIED 89

KIND 91

KING 91

KINGDOM OF GOD 92

LAW 93

LIKENESS (see image also) 94

LORD 95

LOST 95

LOVE 96

LYING/LIE 97

MEDITATE 99

Lord Make It Plain | So I Can Understand - Definitions

MEEK	99
MERCY (don't give me what I do deserve)	100
MIND	100
MINISTER	101
MIRACLE	102
MONEY	104
MOTHER	105
NEED	107
NEVER	108
NEW	108
ORDAINED	111
PATIENCE	113
PEACE/SHALOM (translated as peace)	113
POTENTIAL	114
POVERTY	114
POWER	115
PRAISE	115
PRAY	116
PRAYER (talking with God)	116

PREACH	116
TEACH	117
PRIDE	117
PRIEST	118
PROMISE	119
PROPHET	119
PROSPERITY	120
PROTECT	120
PROTESTANT	121
PROUD	121
PROVIDE	121
RABBI (Teacher)	123
REALITY	123
RECONCILIATION	126
RECONCILE	126
REDEEMED	128
RELIGION	129
RENEW	131
RESPECT	131

RESPONSIBILITY	131
RIGHTEOUSNESS (right standing)	132
SABBATH	133
SACRED	133
SACRIFICE	134
SAINT	136
SALVATION	137
SANCTIFIED	137
SANCTUARY	138
SATAN (The Accuser)	139
SAVIOR	140
SEEK	141
SELFISH	141
SHIELD	141
SHEPHERD	142
SIGHT	143
SIN (missing the mark)	144
SLANDER	147
SLAVE	149

SON OF MAN	150
SOUL	151
SOVEREIGN	153
SPIRIT	154
STEALING	154
STRENGTH	155
SUCCESS	155
TAX COLLECTOR (Publican)	157
THANKSGIVING	158
TITHE	158
TRANSFORM	159
TRINITY	160
TRUTH	161
TRUST	162
VISION	165
WEALTH	167
WISDOM	167
WISE (the ability to apply knowledge)	167
WITCHCRAFT	168

WITNESS	169
WORLD	170
WORD OF GOD	171
WORSHIP	173
BASIC TENETS (BELIEFS) OF CHRISTIANITY	176
APOSTLES CREED	178
OUR NEW COVENANT	180
INDEX	182

James Edward

ABUNDANT

Richly or plentifully supplied; ample. To abound (to be plentiful in number or amount. To be fully supplied, to overflow.

> *For if by the trespass of one man, death reigned through that one man, how much more will those who receive God's ABUNDANT provision of grace and the gift of righteousness reign in life through the one man, Jesus Christ. Romans 5:17*

> *The thief comes only to steal and kill and destroy; I have come so they may have life, and have it more abundantly. John 10:10*

ACKNOWLEDGE

To admit to be real; recognize the existence, truth or fact of. To recognize the authority, validity or claims or to show or express appreciation or gratitude for.

> *Trust in the Lord with all your heart and lean not on your own understanding; in all your ways acknowledge Him and He will make your paths straight.*
> *Proverbs 3:6*

> *Whoever acknowledges Me before me, I will also acknowledge before My Father in heaven. But whoever*

disowns Me before men, I will disown him before My Father in heaven. Matthew 10:32

ADAM

Hebrew ādhām literally, man. The Hebrew word for earth is adama. God formed man from the dust of the earth, and that connection with adama, earth, is the basis for man's name.
Name of the first man on earth. Jesus is also referred to as the Last Adam (see below).

So it is written: "The first man Adam became a living being"; the last Adam, a life-giving spirit. 1 Corinthians 15:45

Then the Lord God formed the man of dust from the ground and breathed into his nostrils the breath of life, and the man became a living creature. Genesis 2:7

The first man was from the earth, a man of dust; the second man is from heaven.
1 Corinthians 15:47

Yet death reigned from Adam to Moses, even over those whose sinning was not like the transgression of Adam, who was a type of the one who was to come. But the free gift is not like the trespass. For if many died through one man's trespass, much more have the grace of God and the free gift by the grace of that one man Jesus Christ abounded for many. And the free gift is not like the result of that one man's sin. For the judgment following one trespass brought condemnation, but the free gift following many trespasses brought justification. For if, because of one man's trespass, death reigned through that one man, much more will those who receive the abundance of grace and the free gift of righteousness reign in life through the one man Jesus Christ. Therefore, as one trespass led to condemnation for all men, so one act of righteousness leads to justification and life for all men. Romans 5:14-21

ADULTERY

Voluntary sexual intercourse between a married person and someone other than his or her lawful spouse.

He who commits adultery lacks sense; he who does it destroys himself. Proverbs 6:32

Flee from sexual immorality. Every other sin a person commits is outside the body, but the sexually immoral person sins against his own body. 1 Corinthians 6:18

For from within, out of the heart of man, come evil thoughts, sexual immorality, theft, murder, adultery. Mark 7:21

ANGELS

A spiritual being believed to act as an attendant, agent, or messenger of God.

Do not neglect to show hospitality to strangers, for thereby some have entertained angels unawares. Hebrews 13:2

Are they not all ministering spirits sent out to serve for the sake of those who are to inherit salvation? Hebrews 1:14

Then the devil left him, and behold, angels came and were ministering to him. Matthew 4:11

AMEN

It is so; so be it (used after a prayer, creed, or other formal statement to express solemn ratification or agreement).
When it occurs at the end of a statement it means agreement with the statement preceding it, such as, "it is truly so" or, "let it be so." Jesus in the Gospels often used the word at the beginning of statements and there it has generally been translated as verily or truly.

> *Blessed be the LORD, the God of Israel, from everlasting even to everlasting Then all the people said, "Amen," and praised the LORD. 1 Chronicles 16:36*

> *...to Him be the glory in the church and in Christ Jesus to all generations forever and ever. Amen. Ephesians 3:21*

> *And blessed be His glorious name forever; And may the whole earth be filled with His glory Amen, and Amen. Psalm 72:19*

> *"For truly I say to you, until heaven and earth pass away, not the smallest letter or stroke shall pass from the Law until all is accomplished. Matthew 5:18*

> *"Truly I say to you, among those born of women there has not arisen anyone greater than John the Baptist! Yet the one who is least in the kingdom of heaven is greater than he. Matthew 11:11*

ANOINT

To rub or sprinkle on; apply an unguent, ointment, or oily liquid to. To smear with any liquid. To consecrate or make sacred in a ceremony that includes the token applying of oil. To dedicate to the service of God.

James Edward

> *It is like precious oil poured on the head, running down on the beard, running down on Aaron's beard, down on the collar of his robe. Psalm 133:2*

> *"The Spirit of the Lord is on me, because he has anointed me to proclaim good news to the poor. He has sent me to proclaim freedom for the prisoners and recovery of sight for the blind, to set the oppressed free. Luke 4:18*

> *"Do not touch my anointed ones; do my prophets no harm." Psalm 105:15*

APOSTLE

Special messenger. Any of the early followers of Jesus who carried the Christian message into the world. The title of the highest ecclesiastical official in certain Protestant sects.
From Greek apostolos meaning a messenger or one sent.

> *And He gave some as apostles, and some as prophets, and some as evangelists, and some as pastors and teachers, for the equipping of the saints for the work of service, to the building up of the body of Christ. Ephesians 4:11-12*

> *With great power the apostles continued to testify to the resurrection of the Lord Jesus. And God's grace was so powerfully at work in them all. Acts 4:33*

ASK

To put a question to; inquire of.

> *"Ask and it will be given to you; seek and you will find; knock and the door will be opened to you. Matthew 7:7*

> *When you ask, you do not receive, because you ask with wrong motives, that you may spend what you get on your pleasures. James 4:3*

AUTHORITY

Power, right to exercise power over someone else.
The right and power to command, enforce laws, determine, influence or judge. A person or group invested with this right and power.
From the Greek exousia the authority or the right to act.

> *All authority in heaven and earth has been given to me. Therefore go and make disciples of all nations, baptizing them in the name of the Father and of the Son and of the Holy Spirit and teaching them to obey everything I have commanded you. And surely I am with you always to the very end of the age. Matthew 28:18*

> *Everyone must submit himself to the governing authorities for there is no authority except that which God has established. The authorities that exist have been established by God. Consequently he who rebels against the authority is rebelling against what God has instituted and those who do so will bring judgment on themselves. Romans 13: 1&2*

B

BAPTISM

A ceremonial immersion in water, or application of water, as an initiatory rite or sacrament of the Christian church. A trying or purifying experience or initiation.
From the Greek baptizo meaning to immerse, submerge or overwhelm.

> *And Peter said to them, Repent and be baptized every one of you in the name of Jesus Christ for the forgiveness of your sins, and you will receive the gift of the Holy Spirit. Acts 2:38*

> *Having been buried with him in baptism, in which you were also raised with him through faith in the powerful working of God, who raised him from the dead. Colossians 2:12*

> *Go therefore and make disciples of all nations, baptizing them in the name of the Father and of the Son and of the Holy Spirit. Matthew 28:19*

> *For as many of you as were baptized into Christ have put on Christ. Galatians 3:27*

BELIEVE

To have confidence in the truth, existence, reliability or value of something.
From the Greek pisteuo (trust) meaning to receive information into one's mind, accept it as being true, and have enough confidence in it to act or be willing to act on it.

"If you can?" said Jesus, "Everything is possible to him who BELIEVES. Mark 9:23

I am the resurrection and the life. He who BELIEVES in me will live, even though he dies; and whoever lives and believes in me will never die. Do you BELIEVE this? John 11:25&26

And without faith it is impossible to please him, for whoever would draw near to God must believe that he exists and that he rewards those who seek him. Hebrews 11:6

For with the heart one believes and is justified, and with the mouth one confesses and is saved. Romans 10:10

BIBLE

The collection of sacred writings of the Christian religion, comprising the Old and New Testaments.
The Bible was written over a 1600 year period by approximately 40 men, most of who never met each other or knew of the others writings. It was written on 3 continents, in 3 languages on the most controversial subjects, by authors whose education and background varied greatly (kings, shepherds, scientists, attorneys, a tax collector, an army general, fishermen, priests, and a physician).
The time of the writing was from 1500 BC to AD 100. While the Bible is 1 book, it contains 66 smaller books. The books of the Old Testament were written before the birth of Jesus the Christ and the New Testament covers the life of Christ and beyond.

All scripture is given by inspiration of God, and is profitable for doctrine, for reproof, for correction, for instruction in righteousness: That the man of God may be perfect,

> thoroughly furnished unto all good works. 2 Timothy 3:16-17
>
> *Your word is a lamp to my feet and a light to my path. Psalm 119:105*
>
> *For whatever was written in former days was written for our instruction, that through endurance and through the encouragement of the Scriptures we might have hope. Romans 15:4*
>
> *Heaven and earth will pass away, but my words will not pass away. Luke 21:33*
>
> *My son, do not forget my teaching, but let your heart keep my commandments, for length of days and years of life and peace they will add to you. Proverbs 3:1-2*

BISHOP (Overseer)

A person who supervises a number of local churches or a diocese, being in the Greek, Roman Catholic, Anglican, and other churches a member of the highest order of the ministry. A spiritual supervisor, overseer, or the like.

From the Greek episkopos meaning epi = upon + skopos = a watcher; one who watches over, an overseer.

> *Be on guard for yourselves and for all the flock, among which the Holy Spirit has made you overseers, to shepherd the church of God which He purchased with His own blood. Acts 20:28*

Now the overseer is to be above reproach, faithful to his wife, temperate, self-controlled, respectable, hospitable, able to teach. 1 Timothy 3:2

And what you have heard from me in the presence of many witnesses entrust to faithful men who will be able to teach others also. 2 Timothy 2:2

BLASPHEME

Slander, insult the honor of, injure the reputation of, say untruths about Him, His name or His word. Impious utterance or action concerning God or sacred things. An act of cursing or reviling God. The crime of assuming to oneself the rights or qualities of God. Irreverent behavior toward anything held sacred, priceless, etc.
From the Greek blasphemeo: blapto = to hurt + phemi = to say; to speak injuriously, contemptuously.

At that time two robbers were crucified with Him, one on the right and one on the left. And those passing by were hurling abuse at Him, wagging their heads and saying, "You who are going to destroy the temple and rebuild it in three days, save Yourself! If You are the Son of God, come down from the cross." Matthew 27:38-39

"Truly I say to you, all sins shall be forgiven the sons of men, and whatever blasphemies they utter; but whoever blasphemes against the Holy Spirit never has forgiveness, but is guilty of an eternal sin "-- because they were saying, "He has an unclean spirit." Mark 3:28-30

But Michael the archangel, when he disputed with the devil and argued about the body of Moses, did not dare pronounce against him a railing judgment, but said, "The

James Edward

> *Lord rebuke you!" But these men revile the things which they do not understand; and the things which they know by instinct, like unreasoning animals, by these things they are destroyed. Woe to them! For they have gone the way of Cain, and for pay they have rushed headlong into the error of Balaam, and perished in the rebellion of Korah. Jude 1:9-10*

BLESS

To pronounce goodness or favor upon them. To request God's divine favor upon or for. To bestow good of any kind upon. To consecrate or sanctify by a religious rite; make or pronounce holy. From the Greek makarios meaning benefit given by God.

BLESSED

Consecrated; sacred; holy; sanctified. Worthy of adoration, reverences or worship. Divinely or supremely favored; fortunate.

> *Blessed is the man who perseveres under trial, because when he has stood the test he will receive the crown of life that God has promised to those who love Him. James 1:2*

> *Bless those who persecute you bless and do not curse. Romans 12:14*

> *"The LORD bless you and keep you; the LORD make his face shine upon you and be gracious to you; the LORD turn his face toward you and give you peace." Numbers 6:24-26*

> *"Bring the whole tithe into the storehouse, that there may be food in my house. Test me in this," says the Lord Almighty, "and see if I will not throw open the floodgates of*

heaven and pour out so much blessing that there will not be room enough to store it." Malachi 3:10

James Edward

C

CAPTIVE

A prisoner. A person who is enslaved or dominated. Made or held prisoner. Kept in confinement.

> *The Spirit of the Lord is upon me because He has anointed Me to preach the gospel to the poor; He has sent Me to heal the brokenhearted. To proclaim liberty to the captives and recovery of sight to the blind. To set as liberty those who are oppressed; to proclaim the acceptable year of the Lord. Luke 4:18 & 19*

> *For I see that you are full of bitterness and captive to sin. Acts 8:23*

CARE

A troubled state of mind; worry or concern. A cause or object of worry or concern.

> *Cast all your cares on Him because He cares for you. 1 Peter 5:7*

> *When I consider your heavens, the work of your fingers, the moon and the stars which you have set in place, what is man that you are mindful of him, the son of man that you care for him? Psalm 8:4*

CAREFUL

Cautious in one's actions.

Be very careful then how you live...not as unwise, but as wise making the most of every opportunity because the days are evil. Ephesians 5:15&16

Be careful for nothing; but in everything by prayer and supplication with thanksgiving let your requests be made known unto God. And the peace of God, which passes all understanding, shall keep your hearts and minds through Christ Jesus. Philippians 4:6-7

CARES

A state of mind in which one is troubled; worry, anxiety, or concern. A cause or object of worry, anxiety, concern, etc.

Put your cares on the Lord, and he will be your support; he will not let the upright man be moved. Psalm 55:22

When I am filled with cares, Your comfort brings me joy. Psalm 94:19

Do not be over-anxious, therefore, about to-morrow, for to-morrow will bring its own cares. Enough for each day are its own troubles. Matthew 6:34

Cast all your cares upon Him because He cares for you. 1 Peter 5:7

CHEERFUL

Characterized by or expressive of good spirits or cheerfulness. Joyful, upbeat, enthusiastic.

James Edward

> *Each one must give as he has decided in his heart, not reluctantly or under compulsion, for God loves a cheerful giver. 2 Corinthians 9:7*

> *A glad heart makes a cheerful face, but by sorrow of heart the spirit is crushed. Proverbs 15:13*

CHEATING

To defraud; swindle. To deceive; influence by fraud.

> *The very fact that you have lawsuits among you means you have been completely defeated already. Why not rather be wronged? Why not rather be cheated? 1 Corinthians 6:7*

> *Whoever walks in integrity walks securely, but he who makes his ways crooked will be found out. Proverbs 10:9*

CHRIST/MESSIAH (Anointed)

The promised and expected deliverer of the Jewish people. Jesus Christ, regarded by Christians as fulfilling this promise and expectation. John 4:25, 26.
Note: Christ (Cristos) the Greek for Messiah is not Jesus' last name it is His title. He is Jesus the Christ meaning the anointed and His anointing.

> *He said to them, "But who do you say that I am?" Simon Peter answered, "You are the Christ, the Son of the living God." And Jesus said to him, "blessed are you, Simon Barjona, because flesh and blood did not reveal this to you, but My Father who is in heaven. Matthew 16:15-17*

> *The woman said to him, "I know that Messiah is coming (he who is called Christ). When he comes, he will tell us all*

things." Jesus said to her, "I who speak to you am he."
John 4:25-26

For the wages of sin is death, but the free gift of God is
eternal life in Christ Jesus our Lord. Romans 6:23

CHURCH (called ones)

A building for public Christian worship. the whole body of Christian believers; Christendom. the whole body of Christian believers; Christendom.
From the Greek ekklesia (ek = out of + klesis = a calling); usually referring to those who have responded to God's call to come out of the world. ekklesia is a collective noun, almost always referring to a community of "called ones;" that is, believers in Jesus.

> ...the church of God which is at Corinth, to those who have been sanctified in Christ Jesus, saints by calling, with all who in every place call on the name of our Lord Jesus Christ, their Lord and ours: 1 Corinthians 1:2

> For I am the least of the apostles and do not even deserve to be called an apostle, because I persecuted the church of God. 1 Corinthians 15:9

COMFORT/COMFORTER

To soothe, console, or reassure, bring solace or cheer to. To make physically comfortable. Relief in affliction; consolation, solace. A person or thing that gives consolation or relief. The Holy Spirit (Third person of the Trinity).

> But the Comforter, who is the Holy Spirit, whom the Father will send in my name, he shall teach you all things, and

> *bring all things to your remembrance, whatsoever I have said unto you. John 14:26*
>
> *Praise be to the God and Father of our Lord Jesus Christ, the Father of compassion and the God of all comfort, who comforts us in all our troubles, so that we can comfort those in any trouble with the comfort we ourselves receive from God. For just as we share abundantly in the sufferings of Christ, so also our comfort abounds through Christ. If we are distressed, it is for your comfort and salvation; if we are comforted, it is for your comfort, which produces in you patient endurance of the same sufferings we suffer. And our hope for you is firm, because we know that just as you share in our sufferings, so also you share in our comfort. 2 Corinthians 1:3-7*

COMPASSION

The deep feeling of sharing the suffering of another: mercy. A feeling of deep sympathy and sorrow for someone struck by misfortune, accompanied by a desire to alleviate the suffering.

> *When he saw the crowds he had compassion on them because they were harassed and helpless like sheep without a shepherd. Matthew 9:36*
>
> *When Jesus landed and saw a large crowd he had compassion on them and healed their sick. Matthew 14:14*
>
> *And the Lord said, "I will cause all my goodness to pass in front of you, and I will proclaim my name, the Lord, in your presence. I will have mercy on whom I will have mercy, and I will have compassion on whom I will have compassion. Exodus 33:19*

CONDEMN

To express an unfavorable or adverse judgment on; indicate strong disapproval of: censure. Toe sentence to punishment, esp. a severe punishment: to condemn a murderer to death. To pronounce to be guilty.

> *Therefore, there is now no condemnation for those who are in Christ Jesus. Romans 8:1*
>
> *Do not judge and you will not be judged. Do not condemn and you will not be condemned. Forgive and you will be forgiven. Luke 6:37*

CONFESS

To own or admit as true. To declare or acknowledge (one's sins), especially to God or a priest in order to obtain absolution. To acknowledge one's belief or faith in; declare adherence to. From the Greek homologeo. Homo (same), logia (word) so "same word". Say the same word God says.
From the Greek homologeo to speak the same thing (homos, "same," lego, "to speak"), "to assent, accord, agree with.

> *Truly I say to you, whatever you bind on earth shall have been bound in heaven; and whatever you loose on earth shall have been loosed in heaven.*
> *"Again I say to you, that if two of you agree on earth about anything that they may ask, it shall be done for them by My Father who is in heaven. For where two or three have gathered together in My name, I am there in their midst." Matthew 18:18-20*

James Edward

> *Whosoever therefore shall confess me before men, him will I confess also before my Father which is in heaven. Matthew 10:32*

> *That if you shall confess with thy mouth the Lord Jesus, and shall believe in your heart that God has raised him from the dead, you shall be saved. Romans 10:9*

> *For it is written, as I live, says the Lord, every knee shall bow to me, and every tongue shall confess to God. Romans 14:11*

CONGREGATION

An assembly of persons brought together for common religious worship.

> *For where two or three are gathered in my name, there am I among them." Matthew 18:20*

> *Saying, "I will tell of your name to my brothers; in the midst of the congregation I will sing your praise." Hebrews 2:12*

> *...not giving up meeting together, as some are in the habit of doing, but encouraging one another--and all the more as you see the Day approaching. Hebrews 10:25*

CONFORM

To act in accordance or harmony: to comply. To act in accord with the prevailing standards, attitudes, practices, etc. of society or a group.

> *Do not conform any longer to the pattern of this world, but be transformed by the renewing of your mind. Then you will be able to test and approve what God's will is – His*

good, pleasing and perfect will.
Romans 12:2

For those whom He foreknew, He also predestined to become conformed to the image of His Son, so that He would be the firstborn among many brethren. Romans 8:29

As obedient children, do not be conformed to the former lusts which were yours in your ignorance. 1 Peter 1:14

CONFIDENCE
Belief in the powers, trustworthiness or reliability of a person or thing. Full trust: reliance.

This is the confidence we have in approaching God: that if we ask anything according to his will, he hears us. And if we know that he hears us – whatever we as – we know that we have what we asked of him. 1 John 5:14

Do not, therefore, fling away your fearless confidence, for it carries a great and glorious compensation of reward. For you have need of steadfast patience and endurance, so that you may perform and fully accomplish the will of God, and thus receive and carry away [and enjoy to the full] what is promised. Hebrews 10:35-36

CONVOCATION
A group of people gathered in answer to a summons; assembly.

CONVOKING
To call together; summon to meet or assemble.

James Edward

> *Speak unto the children of Israel, and say unto them, concerning the feasts of the LORD, which you shall proclaim to be holy convocations, even these are my feasts. Leviticus 23:2*

> *Six days shall work be done: but the seventh day is the Sabbath of rest, a holy convocation; you shall do no work on it: it is the Sabbath of the LORD in all your dwellings. Leviticus 23:3*

CONSECRATE

To make or declare sacred; set apart or dedicate to the service of a deity. To devote or dedicate to some purpose.

> *For the law makes men high priests who have weakness; but the word of the oath, which was since the law, makes the Son, who is consecrated forevermore. Hebrews 7:28*

> *"Consecrate every firstborn male to Me, the firstborn from every womb among the Israelites, both man and animal; it is Mine." Exodus 13:2*

> *Therefore Jesus also suffered and died outside the [city's] gate in order that He might purify and consecrate the people through [the shedding of] His own blood and set them apart as holy [for God]. Hebrews 13:12*

COUNSELOR/COUNSEL

A person who counsels; advisor. Advice: opinion or instruction regarding the judgment or conduct of another.

> *For to us a child is born, to us a son is given and the government will be on his shoulders. And he will be called*

> *Wonderful counselor, Mighty God, Everlasting Father, Prince of Peace. Isaiah 9:6*

> *I have told you these things while I am still with you. But the Helper (Comforter, Advocate, Intercessor—counselor, Strengthener, Standby), the Holy Spirit, whom the Father will send in My name [in My place, to represent Me and act on My behalf], He will teach you all things. And He will help you remember everything that I have told you. John 14:26*

COVENANT

An agreement, usually formal, between two or more persons to do or not do something specified.

Bible
A. the conditional promises made to humanity by God, as revealed in Scripture.
B. the agreement between God and the ancient Israelites, in which God promised to protect them if they kept His law and were faithful to Him.

> *In the same way [He] also [took] the cup, after supper, and said, "This cup is the new covenant in My blood. Do this, as often as you drink it, in remembrance of Me." 1 Corinthians 11:25*

> *He has made us competent to be ministers of a new covenant, not of the letter, but of the Spirit; for the letter kills, but the Spirit produces life. 2 Corinthians 3:6*

> *"The days are coming, declares the Lord, when I will make a new covenant with the people of Israel and with the people of Judah.*
> *It will not be like the covenant I made with their ancestors*

James Edward

> *when I took them by the hand to lead them out of Egypt, because they did not remain faithful to my covenant, and I turned away from them, declares the Lord.*
>
> *This is the covenant I will establish with the people of Israel after that time, declares the Lord. I will put my laws in their minds and write them on their hearts. I will be their God, and they will be my people. No longer will they teach their neighbor, or say to one another, 'Know the Lord,' because they will all know me, from the least of them to the greatest. For I will forgive their wickedness and will remember their sins no more." Hebrews 8:9-12*

CREATOR

A person or thing that creates. The creator, God.

CREATE

To cause to come into being, as something unique.

> *In the beginning God created the heavens and the earth. Genesis 1:1*
>
> *Have you not known? Have you not heard? The everlasting God, the Lord, the Creator of the ends of the earth, does not faint or grow weary; there is no searching of His understanding. Isaiah 4:28*
>
> *For they exchanged the truth of God for a lie, and worshiped and served the creature rather than the Creator, who is blessed forever. Amen. Romans 1:25*

CULT

A particular system of religious worship, especially with reference to its rites and ceremonies. A religion or sect considered to be false, unorthodox, or extremist, with members often living outside of conventional society under the direction of a charismatic leader. An unorthodox sect whose members distort the original doctrines of the religion. In a Christian context, the definition of a cult is, specifically, "a religious group that denies one or more of the fundamentals of biblical truth."

> *While Israel was staying in Shittim, the men began to indulge in sexual immorality with Moabite women, who invited them to the sacrifices to their gods. The people ate the sacrificial meal and bowed down before these gods. So Israel yoked themselves to the Baal of Peor. And the LORD's anger burned against them.*
> *The LORD said to Moses, "Take all the leaders of these people, kill them and expose them in broad daylight before the LORD, so that the LORD's fierce anger may turn away from Israel."*
> *So Moses said to Israel's judges, "Each of you must put to death those of your people who have yoked themselves to the Baal of Peor." Numbers 25:1-5*

CURSE

The expression of a wish that misfortune, evil, doom, etc. Befall someone. An evil or misfortune that has been invoked upon one.

> *Bless those who curse you, pray for those who mistreat you. Luke 6:28*

James Edward

Christ redeemed us from the curse of the law by becoming a curse for us for it is written: "cursed is everyone who is hung on a tree." Galatians 3:13

James Edward

D

DEACON

An appointed or elected officer having variously defined duties. From the Greek diakoneo: to attend to, serve, and provide a service. Sometimes translated deacon or minister.

> *He touched her hand, and the fever left her; and she got up and waited on Him. Matthew 8:15*

> *Then the devil left him, and behold, angels came and were ministering to him. Matthew 4:11*

DEMON

An evil spirit, a fallen angel.
From the Greek daimonion: an evil spiritual being.

> *And the great dragon was thrown down, that ancient serpent, who is called the devil and Satan, the deceiver of the whole world—he was thrown down to the earth, and his angels were thrown down with him. Revelations 12:9*

> *And the angels who did not stay within their own position of authority, but left their proper dwelling, he has kept in eternal chains under gloomy darkness until the judgment of the great day. Jude 6*

> That evening they brought to him many who were oppressed by demons, and he cast out the spirits with a word and healed all who were sick. Matthew 8:16

> And behold, they cried out, "What have you to do with us, O Son of God? Have you come here to torment us before the time?" Matthew 8:29

DENY

To refuse to recognize or acknowledge; disown; disavow; repudiate.

> "But whoever denies Me before men, I will also deny him before My Father who is in heaven. Matthew 10:330

> Jesus said to him, "Truly I say to you that this very night, before a rooster crows, you will deny Me three times." Matthew 26:34

DESIRE

To wish or long for; crave; want. A longing or craving, as for something that brings satisfaction or enjoyment.

> Delight yourself in the LORD; and He will give you the desires of your heart. Psalm 37:4

> But I say, walk by the Spirit, and you will not carry out the desire of the flesh. Galatians 5:16

DOMINION

The power or right of governing and controlling; sovereign authority; rule; control.

> *And God said, Let us make man in our image, after our likeness: and let them have dominion over the fish of the sea, and over the fowl of the air, and over the cattle, and over all the earth, and over every creeping thing that creeps upon the earth. Genesis 1:26*
>
> *All the living creatures of the earth will be filled with fear and terror of you from now on, including all the creatures that fly in the sky, everything that crawls on the ground, and all the fish of the ocean. They've been assigned to live under your dominion. Genesis 9:2*
>
> *Yet You have made him a little lower than God, And You crown him with glory and majesty! You make him to rule over the works of Your hands; You have put all things under his feet. Psalm 8:5-6*
>
> *You have put all things in subjection under his feet "for in subjecting all things to him, He left nothing that is not subject to him but now we do not yet see all things subjected to him. Hebrews 2:8*

DOUBT

To be uncertain about: consider questionable or unlikely. To distrust. To Fear. To be uncertain. A feeling of uncertainty. Distrust or suspicion.

> *"Truly I tell you, if anyone says to this mountain, 'Go, throw yourself into the sea,' and does not doubt in their heart but believes that what they say will happen, it will be done for them. Mark 11:23*

And Jesus answered and said to them, "Truly I say to you, if you have faith and do not doubt, you will not only do what was done to the fig tree, but even if you say to this mountain, 'Be taken up and cast into the sea,' it will happen. Matthew 21:21

But when you ask, you must believe and not doubt, because the one who doubts is like a wave of the sea, blown and tossed by the wind. That person should not expect to receive anything from the Lord. Such a person is double-minded and unstable in all they do. James 1:6

James Edward

E

EARNEST

Serious in intention, purpose or effort; sincerely zealous. Showing depth or feeling. Seriously important; grave.

> *Confess your sins to each other and pray for each other so that you may be healed. The earnest prayer of a righteous person has great power and produces wonderful results.*
>
> *Elijah was a human being, even as we are. He prayed earnestly that it would not rain, and it did not rain on the land for three and a half years. James 5:16 & 17*
>
> *The end of the world is coming soon. Therefore, be earnest and disciplined in your prayers. 1 Peter 4:7*

ELOHIM

God, especially as used in the Hebrew text of the Old Testament. Elohim is the plural form of El or Eloh. It is the first name used for God in the Old Testament. It is a grammatically plural noun for "gods" which supports the belief in a triune God - Father, Son and Holy Spirit.

> *In the beginning God created the heavens and the earth. Genesis 1:1*
>
> *Then God said, "Let us make mankind in our image, in our likeness, so that they may rule over the fish in the sea and the birds in the sky, over the livestock and all the wild*

animals, and over all the creatures that move along the ground." Genesis 1:26

The LORD said, "Behold, they are one people, and they all have the same language. And this is what they began to do, and now nothing which they purpose to do will be impossible for them. "Come, let Us go down and there confuse their language, so that they will not understand one another's speech." So the LORD scattered them abroad from there over the face of the whole earth; and they stopped building the city. Genesis 11:6-8

And the LORD God said, "The man has now become like one of us, knowing good and evil. He must not be allowed to reach out his hand and take also from the tree of life and eat, and live forever." Genesis 3:22

Go therefore and make disciples of all nations, baptizing them in the name of the Father and of the Son and of the Holy Spirit. Matthew 28:19

Now there are varieties of gifts, but the same Spirit; and there are varieties of service, but the same Lord; and there are varieties of activities, but it is the same God who empowers them all in everyone. 1 Corinthians 12:4-6

ENEMY

A person who hates, opposes or fosters harmful designs against another; hostile opponent: adversary.

You have heard that it was said, 'Love your neighbor and hate your enemy. But I tell you, love your enemies and pray for those who persecute you, that you may be children

James Edward

> *of your Father in heaven. He causes his sun to rise on the evil and the good, and sends rain on the righteous and the unrighteous. Matthew 5:43 - 45*

> *Do not suppose that I have come to bring peace to the earth. I did not come to bring peace, but a sword. For I have come to turn a man against his father, a daughter against her mother, a daughter-in-law against her mother-in-law — a man's enemies will be the members of his own house. Matthew 10:34*

ENVY

A feeling of resentful discontent, begrudging admiration or covetousness with regard to another's advantages possessions or attainments; desire for something possessed by another. A longing to possess something awarded to or achieved by another.

> *A heart at peace gives life to the body, but envy rots the bones. Proverbs 14:30*

> *Love is patient, love is kind. It does not envy, it does not boast, it is not proud. 1 Corinthians 13:4*

ETERNAL LIFE

All humans that enter this realm will live forever. The question becomes where they will live that life. You are born into this world destined for Hell in the afterlife because of the choice of your ancestor Adam. However by the grace of God He has provided an alternative which would allow you to life with Him forever.

> *"These will go away into eternal punishment, but the righteous into eternal life." Matthew 25:46*

For God so loved the world that He gave His only begotten Son, that whoever believes in Him shall not perish, but have eternal life. John 3:16

Jesus said to her, "I am the resurrection and the life; he who believes in Me will live even if he dies, and everyone who lives and believes in Me will never die. Do you believe this?" John 11:25-26

"This is eternal life, that they may know You, the only true God, and Jesus Christ whom You have sent." John 17:3

ETERNITY/ETERNAL

Infinite time; duration without beginning or end.

Now this is eternal life: that they know you, the only true God, and Jesus Christ, whom you have sent. John 17:3

And this is the testimony: God has given us eternal life, and this life is in his Son. 1 John 5:11

Your throne was established long ago; you are from all eternity. Psalm 93:2

EVANGELIST

A "good newser". A Protestant minister or layperson who serves as an itinerant or special preacher, especially a revivalist. A preacher of the gospel.

On the next day we left and came to Caesarea, and entering the house of Philip the evangelist, who was one of the seven, we stayed with him. Acts 21:8

James Edward

> *And thus I aspired to preach the gospel, not where Christ was already named, so that I would not build on another man's foundation; but as it is written, "They who had no news of Him shall see, and they who have not heard shall understand."*
> Romans 15:20-21

> **Note**: Though all Christians can evangelize the Holy Spirit especially endows some with the spiritual gift of evangelism.
> *And He gave some as apostles, and some as prophets, and some as evangelists, and some as pastors and teachers,*
> Ephesians 4:11

> *But you, be sober in all things, endure hardship, do the work of an evangelist, fulfill your ministry. 2 Timothy 4:5*

EVIL

Morally wrong or bad; immoral; wicked. Harmful; injurious. Characterized or accompanied by misfortune or suffering; unfortunate; disastrous.

> *Do not be overcome by evil, but overcome evil with good.*
> Romans 12:21

> *For our struggle is not against flesh and blood, but against the rulers, against the authorities, against the powers of this dark world and against the spiritual forces of evil in the heavenly realms. Ephesians 6:12*

> *But the Lord is faithful, and he will strengthen you and protect you from the evil one. 2 Thessalonians 3:3*

James Edward

F

FAIR

Free from bias, dishonesty or injustice. Legitimately sought done, give etc.; proper under the rules.

> *If a king judges the poor with fairness, his throne will always be secure. Proverbs 29:14*
>
> *For the Lord's decrees are just, and everything he does is fair. Psalm 33:4*
>
> *The Lord is merciful and fair; our God is compassionate. Psalm 116:5*

FAITH

Perceiving unseen realities. Confidence or trust in a person or thing.
From the Greek pistis meaning belief, faith, and trust.

> *Now faith is the assurance of things hoped for, the conviction of things not seen. For by it the men of old gained approval.*
>
> *By faith we understand that the worlds were prepared by the word of God, so that what is seen was not made out of things which are visible. By faith Abel offered to God a better sacrifice than Cain, through which he obtained the testimony that he was righteous, God testifying about his gifts, and through faith, though he is dead, he still speaks.*

By faith Enoch was taken up so that he would not see death; and he was not found because God took him up; for he obtained the witness that before his being taken up he was pleasing to God. And without faith it is impossible to please Him, *for he who comes to God must believe that He is and that He is a rewarder of those who seek Him. By faith Noah, being warned* by God *about things not yet seen, in reverence prepared an ark for the salvation of his household, by which he condemned the world, and became an heir of the righteousness which is according to faith.*

By faith Abraham, when he was called, obeyed by going out to a place which he was to receive for an inheritance; and he went out, not knowing where he was going. By faith he lived as an alien in the land of promise, as in a foreign land, dwelling in tents with Isaac and Jacob, fellow heirs of the same promise; for he was looking for the city which has foundations, whose architect and builder is God. By faith even Sarah herself received ability to conceive, even beyond the proper time of life, since she considered Him faithful who had promised. Therefore there was born even of one man, and him as good as dead at that, as many descendants *as the stars of heaven in number, and innumerable as the sand which is by the seashore.*

All these died in faith, without receiving the promises, but having seen them and having welcomed them from a distance, and having confessed that they were strangers and exiles on the earth. For those who say such things make it clear that they are seeking a country of their own. And indeed if they had been thinking of that country *from which they went out, they would have had opportunity to return. But as it is, they desire a better country, that is, a heavenly one. Therefore God is not ashamed to be called their God; for He has prepared a city for them.*

By faith Abraham, when he was tested, offered up Isaac, and he who had received the promises was offering up his only begotten son; it was he to whom it was said, "In Isaac your [n]descendants shall be called." He considered that God is able to raise people even from the dead, from which he also received him back as a type. By faith Isaac blessed Jacob and Esau, even regarding things to come. By faith Jacob, as he was dying, blessed each of the sons of Joseph, and worshiped, leaning on the top of his staff. By faith Joseph, when he was dying, made mention of the exodus of the sons of Israel, and gave orders concerning his bones.

By faith Moses, when he was born, was hidden for three months by his parents, because they saw he was a beautiful child; and they were not afraid of the king's edict. By faith Moses, when he had grown up, refused to be called the son of Pharaoh's daughter, choosing rather to endure ill-treatment with the people of God than to enjoy the passing pleasures of sin, considering the reproach of Christ greater riches than the treasures of Egypt; for he was looking to the reward. By faith he left Egypt, not fearing the wrath of the king; for he endured, as seeing Him who is unseen. By faith he kept the Passover and the sprinkling of the blood, so that he who destroyed the firstborn would not touch them. By faith they passed through the Red Sea as though they were passing through dry land; and the Egyptians, when they attempted it, were drowned.

By faith the walls of Jericho fell down after they had been encircled for seven days. By faith Rahab the harlot did not perish along with those who were disobedient, after she had welcomed the spies in peace.

And what more shall I say? For time will fail me if I tell of Gideon, Barak, Samson, Jephthah, of David and Samuel and the prophets, who by faith conquered kingdoms, performed acts of righteousness, obtained promises, shut the mouths of lions, quenched the power of fire, escaped the edge of the sword, from weakness were made strong, became mighty in war, put foreign armies to flight. Women received back their dead by resurrection; and others were tortured, not accepting their release, so that they might obtain a better resurrection; and others experienced mockings and scourgings, yes, also chains and imprisonment. They were stoned, they were sawn in two, they were tempted, they were put to death with the sword; they went about in sheepskins, in goatskins, being destitute, afflicted, ill-treated (men of whom the world was not worthy), wandering in deserts and mountains and caves and holes in the ground.

And all these, having gained approval through their faith, did not receive what was promised, because God had provided something better for us, so that apart from us they would not be made perfect. Hebrews 11

FALLEN FROM GRACE

This expression isn't in the dictionary however it is often used in Christendom to refer to someone who has committed one of the big 3 sins - adultery, homosexuality, murder or some other sin we think is

James Edward

horrendous[1] and is therefore now not saved anymore.

You are severed from Christ, you who would be justified by the law; you have fallen away from grace. Galatians 5:4

The Galatians had been saved under grace and yet some Jews had come into that church and convinced them to be circumcised also. Paul told pointed out to them that they couldn't mix the Law and Grace and that trying go back under the Law after being saved by Grace was in his words falling from grace.

FATHER

A male parent; the begetter of a child; sire. A man who gives paternal care to others; protector or provider. To take responsibility for. To perform the tasks or duties of a male parent; act paternally.

> *Honor your father and your mother, so that you may live long in the land the Lord your God is giving you. Exodus 20:12*
>
> *A father to the fatherless, a defender of widows is God in his holy dwelling. Psalm 68:5*
>
> *Do not call anyone on earth [who guides you spiritually] your father; for One is your Father, He who is in heaven. Matthew 23:9*

---

[1] I'm being facetious when I say big sins and rank them because actually in God's eyes all sin is sin no big or small ones so they all need to be paid for by the blood of His Son. The Bible makes it clear that the Law is one composite (whole) piece and if you break one part of it you are guilty of all them.

FAVOR

Something done or granted out of goodwill, rather than from justice or for remuneration; a kind act. Friendly or well-disposed regard; goodwill. To show preferential treatment as in doing someone a favor.

From the Greek charis: favor, grace, thanks. An unearned benefit bestowed upon a person or category of people.

> *"The patriarchs became jealous of Joseph and sold him into Egypt. Yet God was with him, and rescued him from all his afflictions, and granted him favor and wisdom in the sight of Pharaoh, king of Egypt, and he made him governor over Egypt and all his household. Acts 7:9-10*

> *For You, O Lord, bless the righteous man [the one who is in right standing with You]; You surround him with favor as with a shield. Psalm 5:12*

> *For His anger is but for a moment, His favor is for life; weeping may endure for a night, but joy comes in the morning. Psalm 30:5*

> *For if by the one man's offense death reigned through the one, much more those who receive abundance of grace and of the gift of righteousness will reign in life through the One, Jesus Christ. Romans 5:17*

FEAR

A distressing emotion aroused by impending danger, evil, pain, etc., whether the threat is real or imagined; the feeling or condition of being afraid.

"So do not fear, for I am with you; do not be dismayed, for I am your God. I will strengthen you and help you; I will uphold you with my righteous right hand." Isaiah 41:10

"Peace is what I leave with you; it is my own peace that I give you. I do not give it as the world does. Do not be worried and upset; do not be afraid." John 14:27

"For God has not given us a spirit of fear, but of power and of love and of a sound mind." 2 Timothy 1:7

"Have I not commanded you? Be strong and courageous. Do not be terrified; do not be discouraged, for the Lord your God will be with you wherever you go." Joshua 1:9

FELLOWSHIP

The family feeling and partnership between Christians. Close relationship, participation with sharing. Friendship, friendliness, neighborliness, amity, familiarity, fellowship.
From the Greek koinania meaning Christian fellowship or communion, with God or, more commonly, with fellow Christians.

For God is faithful through whom you were called into Fellowship with His Son Christ Jesus.
1 Corinthians 1:9

Intimate fellowship with Yahweh [is] for those who fear him, and [he] makes known his covenant to them. Psalm 25:14

God is faithful, by whom ye were called unto the fellowship of his Son Jesus Christ our Lord. 1 Corinthians 1:9

FOOL
A silly or stupid person; one who lacks sense.

> The fool says in his hear, "There is no God." They are corrupt, their deeds are vile; there is no one who does good. Psalm 14:1

> A fool does not delight in understanding, but only wants to show off his opinions. Proverbs 18:2

FORNICATION
Voluntary sexual intercourse between two unmarried persons or two persons not married to each other. Adultery.

> Flee from sexual immorality. All other sins a man commits are outside his body, but he who sins sexually sins against his own body. Do you not know that your body is a temple of the Holy Spirit, who is in you, whom you have received from God? You are not your own; you were bought at a price. Therefore honor God with your body. 1 Corinthians 6:18 -20.

> We should not commit sexual immorality, as some of them did and in one day twenty three thousand of them died. 1 Corinthians 10:8

FORGIVE
To excuse for a fault or offense. To stop feeling anger for or resentment against. To absolve from payment of. To grant pardon for or remission of (an offense, debt, etc.); absolve. To give up all claim on account of; remit (a debt, obligation, etc.). To grant pardon to (a person). To cease to feel resentment against. To cancel an indebtedness or liability of.

For if you forgive men when they sin against you, your heavenly Father will also forgive you. Matthey 6:14

Bear with each other and forgive whatever grievances you may have against one another. forgive as the Lord forgave you. Colossians 3:13

Judge not, and ye shall not be judged: condemn not, and ye shall not be condemned: forgive, and ye shall be forgiven: Luke 6:37

FORSAKEN

Deserted; abandoned; forlorn.

I have been young, and now am old; yet have I not seen the righteous forsaken, nor his seed begging bread. Psalm 37:25

Make sure that your character is free from the love of money, being content with what you have; for He Himself has said, "I will never desert you, nor will I ever forsake you," Hebrews 13:5

About three in the afternoon Jesus cried out in a loud voice, "Eli, Eli, lema sabachthani?" (which means "My God, my God, why have you forsaken me?"). Matthew 27:46

FREE

At liberty; not bound or constrained. Not under obligation or necessity. Not affected by a given condition or circumstance. Exempt. Unobstructed, to rid or release, to disengage, untangle. To liberate.

So if the Son sets you free, you will be free indeed. John 8:36

For you are free, yet you are God's slaves, so don't use your freedom as an excuse to do evil. 1 Peter 2:16

And you will know the truth, and the truth will set you free." John 8:32

James Edward

G

GENEROUS

Liberal in giving or sharing; unselfish. Free from meanness or pettiness.

> *Good will come to him who is generous and lends freely, who conducts his affairs with justice. Psalm 112:5*

> *A generous man will himself be blessed, for he shares his food with the poor. Proverbs 22:9*

GENTILE

Of or relating to any people not Jewish. A heathen or pagan.

> *For I am not ashamed of the gospel, because it is the power of God that brings salvation to everyone who believes: first to the Jew, then to the Gentile. Romans 1:6*

> *But when I saw that they were not straightforward about the truth of the gospel, I said to Cephas in the presence of all, "If you, being a Jew, live like the Gentiles and not like the Jews, how is it that you compel the Gentiles to live like Jews?" "We are Jews by nature and not sinners from among the Gentiles; nevertheless knowing that a man is not justified by the works of the Law but through faith in Christ Jesus, even we have believed in Christ Jesus, so that we may be justified by faith in Christ and not by the works of the Law; since by the works of the Law no flesh will be justified. Galatians 2:14-16*

GENTLE

Kindly; amiable: a gentle manner. Not severe, rough or violent; mile; light: a gentle tap on the arm. Polite, refined, courteous, calm.

> *After the earthquake came a fire, but the Lord was not in the fire. And after the fire came a gentle whisper. 1 Kings 19:12*

> *A gentle answer turns away wrath, but a harsh word stirs up anger. Proverbs 15:1*

> *Take my yoke upon you and learn from me, for I am gentle and humble in heart and you will find rest for your souls. Matthew 11:29*

GLAD

Feeling joy or pleasure; delighted; pleased.

> *I was glad when they said to me, "Let us go to the house of the Lord." Psalm 122:1*

> *This is the day the Lord has made; let us rejoice and be glad in it. Psalm 118:24*

> *I will be glad and rejoice in you; I will sing praise to your name, O Most High. Psalm 9:2*

GLORY

Literally "heavy or weighty". Honor, renown; glory, an especially divine quality, the unspoken.
From the Greek doxa. No English word accurately captures the

meaning of doxa, but magnificence comes close. Honor, praise, respect.

> "I glorified You on the earth, having accomplished the work which You have given Me to do. "Now, Father, glorify Me together with Yourself, with the glory which I had with You before the world was. John 17:4-5

> "But when the Son of Man comes in His glory, and all the angels with Him, then He will sit on His glorious throne. "All the nations will be gathered before Him; and He will separate them from one another, as the shepherd separates the sheep from the goats; Matthew 25:31

> The heavens are telling of the glory of God; And their expanse is declaring the work of His hands. Psalm 19:1

> 'And do not lead us into temptation, but deliver us from evil. [For Yours is the kingdom and the power and the glory forever. Amen.]' Matthew 6:13

GOD

The one Supreme Being, the creator and ruler of the universe.

> I am the LORD, and there is no other, besides me there is no God; I equip you, though you do not know me. Isaiah 45:5

> For there is one God, and one mediator also between God and men, the man Christ Jesus. 1 Timothy 2:5

GOOD

Morally excellent; virtuous; righteous. Satisfactory in quality or quantity. Of high quality. Right, proper, fit. Kind or friendly, honorable or worthy.

> *And do not forget to do good and to share with others, for with such sacrifices God is pleased. Hebrews 13:16*

> *Taste and see that the LORD is good. Oh, the joys of those who take refuge in him! Psalm 34:8*

> *Then Jesus asked them, "Which is lawful on the Sabbath: to do good or to do evil, to save life or to kill?" But they remained silent. Mark 3:4*

GOSPEL (Almost too good to be true news)

The teachings of Jesus and the apostles; the Christian revelation. Something absolutely or unquestionably true.

> *For I am not ashamed of the gospel, because it is the power of God that brings salvation to everyone who believes: first to the Jew, then to the Gentile. Romans 1:16*

> *Now I would remind you, brothers, of the gospel I preached to you, which you received, in which you stand, and by which you are being saved, if you hold fast to the word I preached to you—unless you believed in vain.*

> *For I delivered to you as of first importance what I also received: that Christ died for our sins in accordance with the Scriptures, that he was buried, that he was raised on the third day in accordance with the Scriptures, 1 Corinthians 15:1-4*

> *And this gospel of the kingdom shall be preached in all the world for a witness unto all nations; and then shall the end come. Matthew 24:14*
>
> *The Spirit of the Lord is on me, because he has anointed me to proclaim good news to the poor. He has sent me to proclaim freedom for the prisoners and recovery of sight for the blind, to set the oppressed free. Luke 4:18*
>
> *For Christ did not send me to baptize, but to preach the gospel – not with words or human wisdom, lest the cross of Christ be emptied of its power. 1 Corinthians 1:17*
>
> *By this gospel you are saved, if you hold firmly to the word I preached to you. Otherwise, you have believed in vain. 1 Corinthians 15:2*
>
> *But even if we or an angel from heaven should preach to you a gospel contrary to the one we preached to you, let him be accursed. As we have said before, so now I say again: If anyone is preaching to you a gospel contrary to the one you received, let him be accursed. Galatians 1:8-9*

GOSSIP

Idle talk or rumor, esp. about the private affairs of others.

> *A gossip betrays a confidence, but a trustworthy man keeps a secret. Proverbs 11:13*
>
> *Without wood a fire goes out; without gossip a quarrel dies down. Proverbs 26:20*

GRACE (Do give me what I don't deserve)

Favor or goodwill. A manifestation of favor, especially by a superior. Mercy; clemency; pardon. The freely given, unmerited favor and love of God. The influence or Spirit of God operating in humans. A virtue or excellence of divine origin. The condition of being in God's favor or one of the elect.

Note: Grace means "unmerited [not deserved] favor". Favor's definition is "preferential treatment" so Grace is actually undeserved preferential treatment.

> *For the grace of God has appeared, bringing salvation to all men...Titus 2:11*

> *For if, by the trespass of the one man, death reigned through that one man, how much more will those who receive God's abundant provision of grace and of the gift of righteousness reign in life through the one man, Jesus Christ! Romans 5:17*

> *But the gift is not like the trespass. For if the many died by the trespass of the one man, how much more did God's grace and the gift that came by the grace of the one man, Jesus Christ, overflow to the many! Romans 5:15*

GUILTY

Having committed an offense, crime, violation, or wrong, especially against moral or penal law; justly subject to a certain accusation or penalty; culpable.

> *For whoever keeps the whole law and yet stumbles at just one point is guilty of breaking all of it. James 2:10*

Why, then, was the law given? It was given alongside the promise to show people their sins. But the law was designed to last only until the coming of the child who was promised. God gave his law through angels to Moses, who was the mediator between God and the people. Galatians 3:19

GREED

Excessive or rapacious desire, esp. for wealth or possessions; avarice; covetousness.

A greedy man brings trouble to his family, but he who hates bribes will live. Proverbs 15:27

For of this you can be sure: no immoral, impure or greedy person – such a man is an idolater – has any inheritance in the kingdom of Christ and of God. Ephesians 5:5

James Edward

H

HAPPY/HAPPINESS

Characterized by good fortune. Having, showing or marked by pleasure. Cheerfully willing.

> *A happy heart makes the face cheerful, but heartache crushes the spirit. Proverbs 15:13*

> *David also spoke of this when he described the happiness of those who are declared righteous without working for it: Romans 4:6*

HEAL

To make healthy, whole or sound; restore to health; free from ailment. To repair or reconcile; settle. To free from evil; cleanse, purify.

> *Heal the sick, raise the dead, cleanse those who have leprosy, drive out demons. Freely you have received; freely give. Matthew 10:8*

> *But he was pierced for our transgressions, he was crushed for our iniquities; the punishment that brought us peace was upon him, and by his wounds we are healed. Isaiah 53:5*

HEALTH

Soundness of body or mind; freedom from disease or ailment.

Beloved, I wish above all things that you prosper and be in health, even as your soul prospers. 3 John 1:2

A joyful heart is good medicine, but a crushed spirit dries up the bones. Proverbs 17:22

Heal the sick, raise the dead, cleanse those who have leprosy, drive out demons. Freely you have received; freely give. Matthew 10:8

HEIR

A person who inherits or has a right of inheritance in the property of another following the latter's death.

So you are no longer a slave, but God's child; and since you are his child, God has made you also an heir. Galatians 4:7

Now if we are children, then we are heirs--heirs of God and co-heirs with Christ, if indeed we share in his sufferings in order that we may also share in his glory. Romans 4:17

HELL

Note: not a place for bad people.

HELP

Make it easier for (someone) to do something by offering one's services or resources. The action of helping someone to do something; assistance.

...I will lift up my eyes to the mountains; from where shall my help come? My help comes from the LORD, Who made heaven and earth. Psalm 121:1 & 2

James Edward

> ...*God is our refuge and strength, an ever-present help in trouble. Psalm 46:1*

HIGH PRIEST

A chief priest. The priest ranking above all other priests and the only one permitted to enter the holy of holies.

> *For it is declared: "You are a priest forever, in the order of Melchizedek." Hebrews 7:17*

> *Therefore, since we have a great high priest who has ascended into heaven, Jesus the Son of God, let us hold firmly to the faith we profess. For we do not have a high priest who is unable to empathize with our weaknesses, but we have one who has been tempted in every way, just as we are—yet he did not sin. Let us then approach God's throne of grace with confidence, so that we may receive mercy and find grace to help us in our time of need. Hebrews 4:14-16*

HOLIDAY (holy day)

A day fixed by law or custom on which ordinary business is suspended in commemoration of some event or in honor of some person. From the root holy day meaning a religious feast day especially any of several usually commemorative holy days observed in Judaism. A day on which a religious festival is observed

> *Remember the Sabbath day—keep it holy. Exodus 20:8*
> *These are the fixed feasts of the Lord, to be kept by you as holy days of worship, for making an offering by fire to the Lord; a burned offering, a meal offering, an offering of*

beasts, and drink offerings; everyone on its special day; Leviticus 23:37

Therefore let no one pass judgment on you in questions of food and drink, or with regard to a festival or a new moon or a Sabbath. Colossians 2:16

One person esteems one day as better than another, while another esteems all days alike. Each one should be fully convinced in his own mind. The one who observes the day, observes it in honor of the Lord. The one who eats, eats in honor of the Lord, since he gives thanks to God, while the one who abstains, abstains in honor of the Lord and gives thanks to God. Romans 14:5-6

HOLY (set apart for God)

Specially recognized as or declared sacred by religious use or authority; consecrated. Dedicated or devoted to the service of God, the church, or religion. Saintly; godly; pious; devout. Having a spiritually pure quality. Entitled to worship or veneration as or as if sacred.

But just as he who called you is holy, so be holy in all you do; for it is written: "Be holy, because I am holy." 1 Peter 1:15-16

And one called to another and said: "Holy, holy, holy is the Lord of hosts; the whole earth is full of his glory!" Isaiah 6:3

For I am the Lord who brought you up out of the land of Egypt to be your God. You shall therefore be holy, for I am holy." Leviticus 11:45

And the four living creatures, each of them with six wings, are full of eyes all around and within, and day and night they never cease to say, "Holy, holy, holy, is the Lord God Almighty, who was and is and is to come!" Revelations 4:8

HOLY SPIRIT

Third person in the Godhead. The spirit of God. In the belief of many Christians, one of the three persons in the one God, along with the Father and the Son (Jesus is the Son); the Holy Spirit is also called the Holy Ghost. Jesus promised the Apostles that he would send the Holy Spirit after his Crucifixion and Resurrection. The Spirit came to the disciples of Jesus on Pentecost.

But you will receive power when the Holy Spirit comes on you; and you will be my witnesses in Jerusalem, and in all Judea and Samaria, and to the ends of the earth." Acts 1:8

"But the Helper, the Holy Spirit, whom the Father will send in my name, he will teach you all things and bring to your remembrance all that I have said to you." John 14:26

"Go therefore and make disciples of all nations, baptizing them in the name of the Father and of the Son and of the Holy Spirit." Matthew 28:19

While Peter was still speaking these words, the Holy Spirit came down on all those who heard the message. Acts 10:44

HOMOSEXUAL

Attracted sexually to members of one's own sex.

In the same way the men also abandoned natural relations with women and were inflamed with lust for one another. Men committed indecent acts with other men and received in themselves the due penalty for their perversion. Romans 1:27

Do you not know that the wicked will not inherit the kingdom of God? Do not be deceived: Neither the sexually immoral nor idolaters nor adulterers nor male prostitutes nor homosexual offenders nor thieves nor the greedy nor drunkards nor slanderers nor swindlers will inherit the kingdom of God. 1 Corinthians 6:9 & 10

"Do not practice homosexuality, having sex with another man as with a woman. It is a detestable sin. Leviticus 18:22

HONEST
Honorable in principles, intentions, and actions; upright and fair.

An honest witness does not deceive, but a dishonest witness utters lies. Proverbs 14:5

Finally, brethren, whatsoever things are true, whatsoever things are honest, whatsoever things are just, whatsoever things are pure, whatsoever things are lovely, whatsoever things are of good report; if there be any virtue, and if there be any praise, think on these things. Philippians 4:8

HOPE
The feeling that what is wanted can be had or that events will turn out for the best. To look forward to with desire and reasonable

confidence. To believe, desire, or trust. To feel that something desired may happen.

Our English word hope doesn't do us justice. Our hope is fifty fifty meaning you may get it or not such as "I hope it doesn't rain tomorrow" whereas in the Old and New Testaments the words they translated hope were much more confident.

In the Old Testament the Hebrew word batah has the meaning of confidence, security, and being without care. In the New Testament we have the Greek word elpis meaning joyful, confident expectation of good.

So from both of these we can see that the writers were not hoping maybe so maybe no, but they were confidently waiting for the fulfillment of the promise.

> *Let us hold fast the confession of our hope without wavering, for He who promised is faithful; Hebrews 10:23*
>
> *Now faith is the assurance of things hoped for, the conviction of things not seen. Hebrews 11:1*
>
> *...but in your hearts honor Christ the Lord as holy, always being prepared to make a defense to anyone who asks you for a reason for the hope that is in you; yet do it with gentleness and respect, 1 Peter 3:15*

James Edward

I

IMAGE (see likeness also)

A physical likeness or representation of a person, animal, or thing, photographed, painted, sculptured, or otherwise made visible. A mental representation; idea; conception.

> Then God said, "Let us make man in our image, after our likeness. And let them have dominion over the fish of the sea and over the birds of the heavens and over the livestock and over all the earth and over every creeping thing that creeps on the earth." Genesis 1:26

> He is the image of the invisible God, the firstborn of all creation. Colossians 1:15

> I speak to him audibly and in visions, not in mysteries. If he can gaze at the image of the LORD, why aren't you afraid to speak against my servant Moses?" Numbers 12:8

> And we all, who with unveiled faces contemplate the Lord's glory, are being transformed into his image with ever-increasing glory, which comes from the Lord, who is the Spirit. 2 Corinthians 3:18

INIQUITY

Gross injustice or wickedness. A violation of right or duty; wicked act; sin.
Note: Ok to be honest iniquity was a little confusing to me because I thought it was synonymous with Sin, but actually they are

separate – that's why God says He will be merciful to our iniquities and remember our sins no more in Hebrews 8:10.

Here is an example...if the speed limit says 50 and I don't know it, but I go 55 I am still committing a sin because sin means to miss the mark. Doesn't mean I'm a bad person, I just didn't do what I was supposed to do.
now on the other hand say the speed limit says 5o and I know it, but I choose to go 55; however, when I see the Police Officer I slow down to 50. That is iniquity. I knew it all along and intentionally chose to do it.

Now the great thing is God said He will be merciful (not give us what we do deserve) to our iniquities and our sins He'll remember no more.
This is not because we are good, but because He is good and He already punished our sin and iniquity in Christ. Now does that mean we can just go and sin freely...well in the words of Paul GOD FORBID NO!

> *"For I will be merciful to their iniquities, and I will remember their sins no more." Hebrews 8:12*
>
> *Behold, I was brought forth in iniquity, and in sin did my mother conceive me. Psalm 51:5*
>
> *You were perfect in your ways from the day that you were created, till iniquity was found in you. Ezekiel 28:15*

INVISIBLE

Not visible; not perceptible by the eye. An invisible thing or being. The invisible, the unseen or spiritual world.

James Edward

The Son is the image of the invisible God, the firstborn over all creation. Colossian 1:15

By faith he left Egypt, not fearing the wrath of the king; for he endured, as seeing Him who is unseen. Hebrews 11:27

Now to the King eternal, immortal, invisible, the only God, be honor and glory forever and ever. Amen. 1 Timothy 1:17

For since the creation of the world His invisible attributes, His eternal power and divine nature, have been clearly seen, being understood through what has been made, so that they are without excuse. Romans 1:20

James Edward

J

JEALOUSY

Resentful and envious of someone's success, achievements, advantages, etc. A feeling of resentment that another has gained something that one more rightfully deserves. Watchful in guarding something. Intolerant of unfaithfulness or rivalry.

Note: Ok so why jealousy is a good thing…well here's a story. I love my teenage daughter and I love spending time with her. She wants a smart phone and since I'm such a good dad I break down and get her the latest one.
Well once she has the phone she now ignores me and her mother and stays on the phone day and night not wanting to spend time with the rest of the family like we used too.
Well now since this phone is taking so much of my precious daughters time from me, I HATE THIS PHONE and I'm very jealous of it monopolizing my daughter's time. You see I love her so much that I hate anything that takes her time from me and comes between our relationship. That is an example of Godly jealousy. That is also how God feels when He knows He is the only true God and loves you, but you put other things in His place.

> *I am jealous for you with a godly jealousy. I promised you to one husband, to Christ, so that I might present you as a pure virgin to him. 2 Corinthians 11:2*

You must worship no other gods, for the LORD, whose very name is jealous, is a God who is jealous about his relationship with you. Exodus 34:14

JEW

One of a scattered group of people that traces its descent from the Biblical Hebrews or from postexilic adherents of Judaism; Israelite. Originally the name applied to people from the tribe of Judah.

'Now then, if you will indeed obey My voice and keep My covenant, then you shall be My own possession among all the peoples, for all the earth is Mine. Exodus 19:5

For I am not ashamed of the gospel, for it is the power of God for salvation to everyone who believes, to the Jew first and also to the Greek. Romans 1:16

JOY

A feeling of great pleasure or happiness. A source of pleasure.

Note: Joy differs from happiness in that happiness is a response to external circumstances. Such as I win a million dollars and I'm happy, but eventually I'll go back to my natural state. Joy on the other hand comes from within and is a result from a confident knowing or hope on the inside. This is how we can have joy even when things aren't going our way at the time.

But the fruit of the Spirit is love, joy, peace, patience, kindness, goodness, faithfulness, gentleness, self-control; against such things there is no law. Galatians 5:22 & 23

Nehemiah said, "Go and enjoy choice food and sweet drinks, and send some to those who have nothing prepared. This day is holy to our Lord. Do not grieve, for the joy of the LORD is your strength." Nehemiah 8:10

JUSTICE

The administering of deserved punishment or reward.

> *Here is my servant whom I have chosen, the one I love, in whom I delight; I will put my Spirit on him and he will proclaim justice to the nations.* Matthew 12:18

> *Mighty King, lover of justice, you have established fairness. You have acted with justice and righteousness throughout Israel.* Psalm 99:4

JUSTIFICATION

A reason, fact, circumstance or explanation that justifies. An act of justifying. The act of God whereby humankind is absolved of guilt or sin.

> *Therefore as by the offense of one judgment came upon all men to condemnation; even so by the righteousness of one the free gift came upon all men unto justification of life.* Romans 5:18

> *Through him everyone who believes is set free from every sin, a justification you were not able to obtain under the Law of Moses.* Acts 13:39

JUSTIFY/JUSTIFIED

To show or prove to be just, right or reasonable. To declare innocent or guiltless; absolve; acquit.

Note: A simple way to remember what this word means is "to make just as if I hadn't sinned. Same as Righteous.

Scripture foresaw that God would justify the Gentiles by faith, and announced the gospel in advance to Abraham: "All nations will be blessed through you." Galatians 3:8

After he has suffered, he will see the light of life and be satisfied; by his knowledge my righteous servant will justify many, and he will bear their iniquities. Isaiah 53:11

James Edward

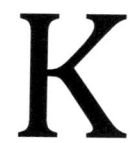

K

KIND

Of a good or benevolent nature or disposition, as a person compassionate, considerate or helpful. Mild; gentle, benign, loving, affectionate.

> *Love is patient, love is kind. It does not envy, it does not boast, it is not proud. 1 Corinthians 13:4*

> *A kind man benefits himself, but a cruel man brings trouble on himself. Proverbs 11:17*

> *Make sure that nobody pays back wrong for wrong, but always try to be kind to each other and to everyone else. 1 Thessalonians 5:15*

KING

A male sovereign or monarch; a man who holds by life tenure, and usually by hereditary right, the chief authority over a country and people. God or Christ.

> *...which He will bring about at the proper time--He who is the blessed and only Sovereign, the King of kings and Lord of lords, 1 Timothy 6:15*

> *And on His robe and on His thigh He has a name written, "King of Kings, And Lord of Lords." Revelations 19:16*

He has made us a Kingdom of priests for God his Father. All glory and power to him forever and ever! Amen.
Revelations 1:6

KINGDOM OF GOD

Christ's mediatorial (of, relating to, or characteristic of a mediator) authority, or his rule on the earth; the blessings and advantages of all kinds that flow from this rule; the subjects of this kingdom taken collectively, or the Church.

But seek ye first the kingdom of God, and his righteousness; and all these things shall be added unto you. Matthew 6:11

...for the kingdom of God is not eating and drinking, but righteousness and peace and joy in the Holy Spirit. Romans 14:17

Heal the sick who are there and tell them, 'The kingdom of God has come near to you.' Luke 10:9

L

LAW

The principles and regulations established in a community by some authority and applicable to its people, whether in the form of legislation or of custom and policies recognized and enforced by judicial decision.

Judaism a law or body of laws derived from the Torah in accordance with interpretations (the Oral Law) traditionally believed to have been given to Moses on Mount Sinai together with the Written Law.

The body of laws contained in the first five books of the Old Testament; Pentateuch.

Note: we normally refer to the Ten Commandments, but there are actually 613 mitzvot (commandments) broken into three categories covering all areas of life such as Marriage, Divorce and Family, Times and Seasons and Holidays to name a few.

> *But if the ministry of death, written and engraved on stones, was glorious, so that the children of Israel could not look steadily at the face of Moses because of the glory of his countenance, which glory was passing away, how will the ministry of the Spirit not be more glorious? For if the ministry of condemnation had glory, the ministry of righteousness exceeds much more in glory. 2 Corinthians 3:7-9*

> *For no one can ever be made right with God by doing what the law commands. The law simply shows us how sinful we are. Romans 3:20*
>
> *...because the law brings about wrath; for where there is no law there is no transgression. Romans 4:15*
>
> *For whoever keeps the whole law but fails in one point has become accountable for all of it. James 2:10*
>
> *The sting of death is sin, and the power of sin is the law. 1 Corinthians 15:56*

LIKENESS (see image also)

A representation, picture, or image, especially a portrait. The state or fact of being like. Resemblance, similitude. shape, form.

> *And God said, Let us make man in our image, after our likeness: and let them have dominion over the fish of the sea, and over the fowl of the air, and over the cattle, and over all the earth, and over every creeping thing that creepeth upon the earth. Genesis 1:26*
>
> *Just as we have borne the likeness of the man who was made from dust, we will also bear the likeness of the man from heaven. 1 Corinthians 15:49*
>
> *Therefore we all, beholding as in a glass the glory of the Lord with uncovered face, are transformed from glory to glory into the same likeness, even as by the Spirit of the Lord. 2 Corinthians 3:18*

> *[Now] He is the exact likeness of the unseen God [the visible representation of the invisible]; He is the Firstborn of all creation. Colossians 1:15*
>
> *He is the reflection of God's glory and the exact likeness of his being, and he holds everything together by his powerful word. After he had provided a cleansing from sins, he sat down at the right hand of the Highest Majesty. Hebrews 1:3*

LORD

A person who has authority, control, or power over others; a master, chief, or ruler. (with capital L meaning) the Supreme Being; God; Jehovah. (with capital L meaning) the Savior, Jesus Christ.
Note: Lower case lord is a human ruler. Capital L Lord is a reference to one of the Persons of the Godhead, Father, Son or Holy Spirit or it may be referring to all three. When you see the term entirely capitalized — LORD — it will be in the Old Testament and is translating the Hebrew word for the name of God — YHWH, or Yahweh (English Jehovah).

> *The LORD is my strength and my defense; he has become my salvation. Psalm 118:14*
>
> *Finally, be strong in the Lord and in his mighty power. Ephesians 6:10*
>
> *"The LORD is my light and my salvation; whom shall I fear? The LORD is the strength of my life; of whom shall I be afraid?" Psalm 27:1*

LOST

No longer possessed. Having gone astray. Destroyed; ruined.

For the Son of Man came to see and to save what was lost. Luke 19:10

This happened so that the words he had spoken would be fulfilled: "I have not lost one of those you gave me." John 18:9

LOVE

Intense affection and warm feeling for another. A strong feeling of fondness or enthusiasm.

Note: The Greeks had several words for love depending on the relationship with the other.

> **Eros** – from where we get our word erotic or sexual passion
>
> **Phileo** - deep friendship, brotherly love, sacrifice between friends.
>
> **Storge** – this is another type of phileo, but embodies the love between a parent and their child.
>
> **Ludus** - playful love encompassing the love between children or young lovers. Flirting or teasing.
>
> **Agape** – selfless love for everyone also the love of God for man and of man for God.. Later translated into Latin as caritas which is where we get our word charity.
>
> **Pragma** - longstanding love. Patient, sacrificial understanding developed between long married couples.

> **Philautia** - love of ones self. Can be good and healthy or it can take on negative tendencies leading to narcissism and selfishness.

> *Love is patient, love is kind. It does not envy, it does not boast, it is not proud. It does not dishonor others, it is not self-seeking, it is not easily angered, it keeps no record of wrongs. Love does not delight in evil but rejoices with the truth. It always protects, always trusts, always hopes, always perseveres. Love never fails. 1 Corinthians 13:4 - 8*

> *For God so loved the world that he gave his one and only son, that whoever believes in him shall not perish, but have eternal life. John 3:16*

LYING/LIE

A false statement made with deliberate intent to deceive; a falsehood. Something intended to convey a false impression; imposture.

> *There are six things the Lord hates, seven that are detestable to him: haughty eyes, a lying tongue, hands that shed innocent blood, a heart that devises wicked schemes, feet that are quick to rush into evil, a false witness who pours out lies and a person who stirs up conflict in the community. Proverbs 6:16 - 19*

> *God did this so that, by two unchangeable things in which it is impossible for God to lie, we who have fled to take hold of the hope set before us may be greatly encouraged. Hebrews 6:18*

Not at all! Let God be true, and every human being a liar. As it is written: "So that you may be proved right when you speak and prevail when you judge." Romans 3:4

James Edward

M

MEDITATE

From the Hebrew Hagah meaning to: mutter, imagine, meditate, mourn, roar, speak, study. Think of going over something over and over and then over again to get a full understanding of it. Also to engage in thought or contemplation; reflect.

> *"This book of the law shall not depart from your mouth, but you shall meditate on it day and night, so that you may be careful to do according to all that is written in it; for then you will make your way prosperous, and then you will have success. Joshua 1:8*
>
> *Sing ye to Him, sing psalms to Him, Meditate on all His wonders. 1 Chronicles 16:9*
>
> *Meditate upon these things; give yourself wholly to them; that your progress may appear to all. 1 Timothy 4:15*
>
> *On the glorious splendor of Your majesty And on Your wonderful works, I will meditate. Psalm 145:5*

MEEK

Humble patient or docile, as under provocation from others. Having the right or the power to do something but refraining for the benefit of someone else. Power under control.

> *Blessed are the meek, for they shall inherit the earth. Matthew 5:5*

Now the man Moses was very meek, more than all people who were on the face of the earth. Numbers 12:3

Take my yoke upon you and learn from me, for I am gentle and humble in heart, and you will find rest for your souls. Matthew 11:29

MERCY (don't give me what I do deserve)

Compassionate or kindly forbearance shown toward and offender, an enemy or other person in one's power; compassion, pity or benevolence. The disposition or discretionary power to be compassionate or forbearing. An act of kindness, compassion or favor.

But go and learn what this means: 'I desire mercy, not sacrifice.' For I have not come to call the righteous, but sinners." Matthew 9:13

May God give you more and more mercy, peace, and love. Jude 1:2

But God had mercy on me so that Christ Jesus could use me as a prime example of his great patience with even the worst sinners. Then others will realize that they, too, can believe in him and receive eternal life. 1 Timothy 1:16

MIND

The element, part, substance, or process that reasons, thinks, feels, wills, perceives, judges, etc.

The LORD said, "Look! They are one people with the same language for all of them, and this is only the beginning of what they will do. Nothing that they have a mind to do will be impossible for them! Genesis 11:6

Set your minds on things that are above, not on things that are on earth. Colossians 3:2

Those who live according to the flesh have their minds set on what the flesh desires; but those who live in accordance with the Spirit have their minds set on what the Spirit desires. Romans 8:5

For the mind-set of the flesh is death, but the mind-set of the Spirit is life and peace. Romans 8:6

"'For who has understood the mind of the Lord so as to instruct him?' But we have the mind of Christ." Corinthians 2:16

"Do not be conformed to this world, but be transformed by the renewal of your mind, that by testing you may discern what is the will of God, what is good and acceptable and perfect." Romans 12:2

"For this is the covenant that I will make with the house of Israel after those days, declares the Lord: I will put my laws into their minds, and write them on their hearts, and I will be their God, and they shall be my people." Hebrews 8:10

MINISTER

A person authorized to conduct religious worship; member of the clergy; pastor. To give service, care, or aid; attend, as to wants or necessities: to help.

Then the devil left Him; and behold, angels came and began to minister to Him. Matthew 4:11

Are they not all ministering spirits, sent forth to minister for them who shall be heirs of salvation?

But it shall not be so among you: but whosoever will be great among you, let him be your minister. Matthew 20:26

Even as the Son of man came not to be ministered unto, but to minister, and to give his life a ransom for many. Matthew 20:28

MIRACLE

An effect or extraordinary event in the physical world that surpasses all known human or natural powers and is ascribed to a supernatural cause. Such an effect or event manifesting or considered as a work of God. A wonder; marvel.
From the Greek dunamis meaning to have ability, or to have superhuman power. Physical power, force, might, ability, efficacy, energy, powerful deeds, deeds showing (physical) power, marvelous works.

> *"Now to him who is able to do immeasurably more than all we ask or imagine, according to his power that is at work within us, to him be glory in the church and in Christ Jesus throughout all generations, forever and ever! Amen" Ephesians 3:20-21*
>
> *"He performs wonders that cannot be fathomed, miracles that cannot be counted" (Job 5:9*

"I am the Lord, the God of all mankind. Is anything too hard for me?" (Jeremiah 32:27

When I was with you, I certainly gave you proof that I am an apostle. For I patiently did many signs and wonders and miracles among you. 2 Corinthians 12:12

And so he did only a few miracles there because of their unbelief. Matthew 13:58

"'If you can'?" said Jesus. "Everything is possible for one who believes."

Mark 9:23

Taking the five loaves and the two fish and looking up to heaven, he gave thanks and broke them. Then he gave them to the disciples to distribute to the people. They all ate and were satisfied, and the disciples picked up twelve basketfuls of broken pieces that were left over.

Luke 9:16-17

And all the more believers in the Lord, multitudes of men and women, were constantly added to their number, to such an extent that they even carried the sick out into the streets and laid them on cots and pallets, so that when Peter came by at least his shadow might fall on any one of them. Also the people from the cities in the vicinity of Jerusalem were coming together, bringing people who were sick or afflicted with unclean spirits, and they were all being healed. Acts 5:14-16

But you will receive power when the Holy Spirit comes on you; and you will be my witnesses in Jerusalem, and in all Judea and Samaria, and to the ends of the earth." Acts 1:8

But if the Spirit of Him who raised Jesus from the dead dwells in you, He who raised Christ Jesus from the dead will also give life to your mortal bodies through His Spirit who dwells in you. Romans 8:11

MONEY

Any circulating medium of exchange, including coins, paper money and demand deposits.

For the love of money is a root of all kinds of evil. Some people, eager for money, have wandered from the faith and pierced themselves with many griefs. 1 Timothy 6:10

The officials make a feast for enjoyment [instead of repairing what is broken], and serve wine to make life merry, and money is the answer to everything. Ecclesiastes 10:19

"Show Me a denarius. Whose likeness and inscription does it have?" They said, "Caesar's." And He said to them, "Then render to Caesar the things that are Caesar's, and to God the things that are God's." Luke 20:24-25

"And my God will meet all your needs according to his glorious riches in Christ Jesus." Philippians 4:19

""Bring the whole tithe into the storehouse, that there may be food in my house. Test me in this,' says the LORD Almighty, "and see if I will not throw open the floodgates of

James Edward

> *heaven and pour out so much blessing that you will not have room enough for it.'" Malachi 3:10*
>
> *"The rich rule over the poor, and the borrower is servant to the lender." Proverbs 22:7*

MOTHER

A female parent.

> *Honor your father and your mother, so that you may live long in the land the Lord your God is giving you. Exodus 20:12*
>
> *Then the man--Adam--named his wife Eve, because she would be the mother of all who live. Genesis 3:20*

James Edward

N

NEED

A lack of something wanted or deemed necessary. To have need of; require as in "I need money".

> *"And my God will meet all your needs according to his glorious riches in Christ Jesus." Philippians 4:19*
>
> *"And when you are praying, do not use meaningless repetition as the Gentiles do, for they suppose that they will be heard for their many words. "So do not be like them; for your Father knows what you need before you ask Him. "Pray, then, in this way: 'Our Father who is in heaven, Hallowed be Your name. Matthew 6:7-9*
>
> *Look at the birds of the air, for they neither sow nor reap nor gather into barns; yet your heavenly Father feeds them. Are you not of more value than they? Which of you by worrying can add one cubit to his stature?*
>
> *"So why do you worry about clothing? Consider the lilies of the field, how they grow: they neither toil nor spin; and yet I say to you that even Solomon in all his glory was not arrayed like one of these. Now if God so clothes the grass of the field, which today is, and tomorrow is thrown into the oven,* will He *not much more* clothe *you, O you of little faith?*

"Therefore do not worry, saying, 'What shall we eat?' or 'What shall we drink?' or 'What shall we wear?' For after all these things the Gentiles seek. For your heavenly Father knows that you need all these things. But seek first the kingdom of God and His righteousness, and all these things shall be added to you. Therefore do not worry about tomorrow, for tomorrow will worry about its own things. Sufficient for the day is its own trouble. Matthew 6:26-34

NEVER

Not ever; at no time: "the idea never occurred to me". Not at all; absolutely not.

Let your character [your moral essence, your inner nature] be free from the love of money [shun greed—be financially ethical], being content with what you have; for He has said, "I will never [under any circumstances] desert you [nor give you up nor leave you without support, nor will I in any degree leave you helpless], nor will I forsake or let you down or relax My hold on you [assuredly not]!" Hebrews 13:5

Rejoice always, pray without ceasing, give thanks in all circumstances; for this is the will of God in Christ Jesus for you. 1 Thessalonians 5:16-18

NEW

Of recent origin, production, purchase, etc.; having but lately come or been brought into being. Of a kind new appearing for the first time. Having but lately or but now become known. Never existed before.

James Edward

Therefore, if anyone is in Christ, he is a new creation; the old has gone, the new has come! 2 Corinthians 5:17

See, I am doing a new thing! Now it springs up; do you not perceive it? I am making a way in the wilderness and streams in the wasteland. Isaiah 43:19

Therefore if anyone is in Christ, he is a new creature; the old things passed away; behold, new things have come. 2 Corinthians 5:17

O

ORDAINED

To invest with ministerial or sacerdotal functions; confer holy orders upon. To select for or appoint to an office.

> *Put these on your brother Aaron and his sons; then anoint, ordain, and consecrate them, so that they may serve Me as priests. Exodus 28:41*
>
> *Even so did the Lord ordain that they that proclaim the gospel should live of the gospel. 1 Corinthians 9:14*
>
> *Do not ordain anyone hastily. Do not participate in the sins of others. Keep yourself pure. 1 Timothy 5:22*

James Edward

P

PATIENCE

The bearing of provocation, annoyance, misfortune or pain without complaint, loss of temper or anger. An ability or willingness to suppress restlessness or annoyance when confronted with delay. Quiet, steady perseverance; even-tempered care; diligence.

> *Love is patient, love is kind and is not jealous; love does not brag and is not arrogant, 1 Corinthians 13:4*
>
> *The Lord is not slow in keeping his promise, as some understand slowness. Instead he is patient with you, not wanting anyone to perish, but everyone to come to repentance. 2 Peter 3:9*
>
> *We do not want you to become lazy, but to imitate those who through faith and patience inherit what has been promised. Hebrews 6:12*
>
> *A man's wisdom gives him patience; it is to his glory to overlook an offense. Proverbs 19:11*

PEACE/SHALOM (translated as peace)

The Hebrew word shalom was translated as peace over two hundred times in the Bible. This really doesn't do this word justice because we know peace as "cessation of or freedom from any strife or dissension.", but shalom is so much deeper.
It is packed with much more depth meaning peace, yes, but also harmony, completeness, safety, soundness of body, welfare, health,

prosperity, quiet, tranquility, contentment, peace in human relationships & peace with God.
Shalom also includes the idea of vigor and vitality in all dimensions of life. In short, shalom speaks of holistic ("holy") health for our souls and spirits.
It is also used as a greeting for both hello and goodbye

> *Shalom I leave with you. My shalom I give to you; not as the world gives, give I to you. Don't let your heart be troubled, neither let it be fearful. John 14:27*

> *The Lord will give strength to His people; the Lord will bless His people with peace. Psalm 29:11*

> *The steadfast of mind You will keep in perfect peace, because he trusts in You. Isaiah 26:3*

POTENTIAL

Capable of being but not yet realized; latent. Capacity for growth, development or progress.

> *For I know the plans I have for you, declares the Lord, plans to prosper you and not to harm you, plans to give you hope and a future. Jeremiah 29:11*

> *But, as it is written, "What no eye has seen, nor ear heard, nor the heart of man imagined, what God has prepared for those who love him". 1 Corinthians 2:9*

POVERTY

The state or condition of having little or no money, goods or means of support; condition of being poor; indigence.

James Edward

> *For you know the grace of our Lord Jesus Christ, that though he was rich, yet for your sakes he became poor, so that you through his poverty might become rich. 1 Corinthians 8:9*
>
> *All hard work brings a profit, but mere talk leads only to poverty. Proverbs 14:23*
>
> *One man gives freely, yet gains even more; another withholds unduly, but comes to poverty. Proverbs 11:24*

POWER

Ability to do or act; capability of doing or accomplishing something. Great or marked ability to do or act; strength; might; force. The possession of control or command over others; authority; ascendancy.
From the Greek dunamis meaning power to do something by super-human means, or the super-human deeds themselves – miracles.

PRAISE

The act of expressing approval or admiration; commendation. The offering of grateful homage in words or song as an act of worship.

> *But you are holy, O you that inhabit the praises of Israel. Psalm 22:3*
>
> *Praise the LORD. Praise God in his sanctuary; praise him in his mighty heavens. Psalm 150:1*
>
> *I will bless the Lord at all times: his praise shall continually be in my mouth. Psalm 34:1*

PRAY

To offer devout petition, praise, thanks, etc.; to (God or an object of worship). Ask, intercession, plead, beg, praise, thank.

PRAYER (talking with God)

A devout petition to God or an object of worship. A spiritual communion with God or an object of worship, as in supplication, thanksgiving or adoration.

> *One day soon afterward Jesus went up on a mountain to pray, and he prayed to God all night. Luke 6:12*

> *But Jesus often withdrew to lonely places and prayed. Luke 5:16*

> *Never stop praying. 1 Thessalonians 5:17*

> *Therefore confess your sins to each other and pray for each other so that you may be healed. The prayer of a righteous person is powerful and effective. James 5:16*

> *...if my people, who are called by my name, will humble themselves and pray and seek my face and turn from their wicked ways, then I will hear from heaven, and I will forgive their sin and will heal their land. 2 Chronicles 7:14*

> *So do not be like them [praying as they do]; for your Father knows what you need before you ask Him. Matthew 6:8*

PREACH

To proclaim, deliver or make known by sermon the gospel, good tidings, etc. To herald or announce the good news.

James Edward

From the Greek euangelion: eu good + angelia = message, announcement, news; thus, good message, good news or gospel.

TEACH

To impart knowledge of or skill in; give instruction in: inform, enlighten, discipline, drill, school, indoctrinate; coach.

From the Greek didasko: to impart information, explain, to teach, be a teacher.

Note: Generally we preach to the unsaved to call them in and teach or train up those in the body. In the New Testament the terms were used interchangeably, but technically preaching lays the foundation for teaching, just as an announcement lays the foundation for further comments.

A good example (not perfect, but close) of this would be John the Baptist and Jesus Himself. John was a Preacher and he announced the good news of the coming Christ while Jesus taught His disciples and in the Synagogues.

> *Now in those days John the Baptist came, preaching in the wilderness of Judea, saying, "Repent, for the kingdom of heaven is at hand." Matthew 3:1*

> *Jesus was going throughout all Galilee, teaching in their synagogues and proclaiming the [a]gospel of the kingdom, and healing every kind of disease and every kind of sickness among the people. Matthew 4:23*

PRIDE

The state or quality of being proud. A high or inordinate opinion of one's own importance or superiority; conceit.

But he gives us more grace. That is why Scripture says: "God opposes the proud but shows favor to the humble." James 4:6

Do nothing out of selfish ambition or vain conceit. Rather, in humility value others above yourselves… Philippians 2:3

Pride goes before destruction, a haughty spirit before a fall. Proverbs 16:18

PRIEST

A person whose office it is to perform religious rites, and especially to make sacrificial offerings. **Note**: the Priest speaks to God on behalf of the people.

But you are a chosen race, a royal priesthood, a holy nation, a people for his own possession, that you may proclaim the excellencies of him who called you out of darkness into his marvelous light. 1 Peter 2:9

And you have made them a kingdom and priests to our God, and they shall reign on the earth." Revelations 5:10

The LORD has sworn and will not change His mind, "You are a priest forever According to the order of Melchizedek." Psalm 110:4

For it was fitting for us to have such a high priest, holy, innocent, undefiled, separated from sinners and exalted above the heavens; Hebrews 7:26

James Edward

PROMISE

A declaration that something will or will not be done, given, etc., by one. Something that has the effect of an express assurance; indication of what may be expected.

> *For the promise is unto you, and to your children, and to all that are afar off, even as many as the Lord our God shall call. Acts 2:39*

> *For the promise, that he should be the heir of the world, was not to Abraham, or to his seed, through the law, but through the righteousness of faith. For if they which are of the law be heirs, faith is made void, and the promise made of none effect: Romans 4:13-14*

> *He staggered not at the promise of God through unbelief; but was strong in faith, giving glory to God; and being absolutely certain that whatever promise He is bound by He is able also to make good. Romans 4:20-21*

PROPHET

A person who speaks for God or a deity, or by divine inspiration. A person chosen to speak for God and to guide the people of Israel. a person who foretells or predicts what is to come.
Note: the Prophet speaks to the people on behalf of God.

> *"Do not touch my anointed ones; do my prophets no harm." Psalm 105:15*

> *Whoever welcomes a prophet as a prophet will receive a prophet's reward, and whoever welcomes a righteous person as a righteous person will receive a righteous person's reward. Matthew 10:41*

> *"When a prophet speaks in the name of the LORD, if the thing does not come about or come true, that is the thing which the LORD has not spoken. The prophet has spoken it presumptuously; you shall not be afraid of him. Deuteronomy 18:22*

> *For we know in part and we prophesy in part, 1 Corinthians 13:9*

> *But the word of the prophet gives men knowledge and comfort and strength. 1 Corinthians 14:3*

PROSPERITY
A successful, flourishing thriving condition, esp. in financial respects; good fortune.

> *Misfortune pursues the sinner, but prosperity is the reward of the righteous. Proverbs 13:21*

> *Keep this Book of the Law always on your lips; meditate on it day and night, so that you may be careful to do everything written in it. Then you will be prosperous and successful. Joshua 1:8*

PROTECT
To defend or guard from attack, invasion, loss, insult, etc., cover; shield. To provide or be capable of providing protection.

> *The Lord says, "I will rescue those who love me. I will protect those who trust in my name. Psalm 91:14*

> *My prayer is not that you take them out of the world but that you protect them from the evil one. John 17:15*

James Edward

PROTESTANT
Any Western Christian who is not an adherent of a Catholic, Anglican, or Eastern Church.

PROUD
Feeling pleasure or satisfaction over something regarded as honorable or creditable to oneself. Having or showing an inordinate opinion of one's own dignity, superiority, etc.; arrogant; haughty.

> *pride goes before destruction, a haughty spirit before a fall. Proverbs 16:18*

> *But he gives us more grace. That is why scripture says: God opposes the proud but gives grace to the humble. James 4:6*

PROVIDE
To furnish; supply. To make available; afford. To set down as or make a stipulation. To take measures in preparation: provide against emergencies. To supply means of subsistence (existence): provide for one's family.

> *Anyone who does not provide for their relatives, and especially for their own household, has denied the faith and is worse than an unbeliever. 1 Timothy 5:8*

> *And my God will meet all your needs according to the riches of his glory in Christ Jesus. Philippians 4:19*

> *Command those who are rich in this present world not to be arrogant nor to put their hope in wealth, which is so*

uncertain, but to put their hope in God, who richly provides us with everything for our enjoyment. 1 Timothy 6:17

R

RABBI (Teacher)

The chief religious official of a synagogue, trained usually in a theological seminary and duly ordained, who delivers the sermon at a religious service and performs ritualistic, pastoral, educational, and other functions in and related to his or her capacity as a spiritual leader of Judaism and the Jewish community.
A title of respect for a Jewish scholar or teacher. A Jewish scholar qualified to rule on questions of Jewish law.

> *Jesus turned around and saw them following and said to them, "What do you want?" So they said to him, "Rabbi" (which is translated Teacher), "where are you staying?" John 1:38*

> *But He Himself was in the stern asleep, with His head on the cushion: so they woke Him. "Rabbi," they cried, "is it nothing to you that we are drowning?" Mark 4:38*

> *...this man came to Jesus by night and said to Him, "Rabbi, we know that You have come from God as a teacher; for no one can do these signs that You do unless God is with him." John 3:2*

REALITY

The state or quality of being real. Something that exists independently of ideas concerning it. Something that exists independently of all other things and from which all other things derive.

Note: the Bible says God is the invisible God, not the nonexistent God.
In this world we have a saying "I'll believe it when I see it." That is exactly opposite of God's way. He says believe it THEN you'll see it.
Jesus told Thomas that blessed were those who have not seen and yet believe.

Personally I would like to see God with my eyes; however, He didn't setup the system that way so it is incumbent on me to learn that rules and play by them and when I get to Heaven I'll ask Him why He did it this way.

See also 2 Kings 6:17 where Elisha prayed for God to open his servant's eyes and when they were he saw they were surrounded by chariots of fire and Angels.
The important this in the Angels didn't appear when Elisha prayed. They were already there and it was just revealed to his servant so that he would believe, much like Thomas.

I don't know why it is so hard for us to believe in things we can't see because it's a fact that as you read this you are missing about 99% of what is going on around you. You can't see radio waves, TV waves, microwaves, sun rays, sound, your breath, the wind, brain waves, ultra violet light and I could go on and on.
Just Google the visible light spectrum and you'll see that we as humans can't see 99 percent of what we know is there out there and yet we still trust so much in our sight.

> *For from Him [all things originate] and through Him [all things live and exist] and to Him are all things [directed]. To Him be glory and honor forever! Amen. Romans 11:36*

> *In the beginning [before all time] was the Word (Christ), and the Word was with God, and the Word was God*

James Edward

Himself. He was [continually existing] in the beginning [co-eternally] with God. All things were made and came into existence through Him; and without Him not even one thing was made that has come into being. John 1:1 – 3

God is spirit [the Source of life, yet invisible to mankind], and those who worship Him must worship in spirit and truth. John 4:24

He is the exact living image [the essential manifestation] of the unseen God [the visible representation of the invisible], the firstborn [the preeminent one, the sovereign, and the originator] of all creation. Colossian 1:15

Now to the King of the ages [eternal], immortal, invisible, the only God, be honor and glory forever and ever. Amen. 1 Timothy 1:17

Jesus Appears to Thomas
John 20:24 - 29

Now Thomas (also known as Didymusa), one of the Twelve, was not with the disciples when Jesus came. So the other disciples told him, "We have seen the Lord!"

But he said to them, "Unless I see the nail marks in his hands and put my finger where the nails were, and put my hand into his side, I will not believe."

A week later his disciples were in the house again and Thomas was with them. Though the doors were locked, Jesus came and stood among them and said, "Peace be with you!" Then he said to Thomas, "Put your finger here; see my hands. Reach out your hand and put it into my side. Stop doubting and believe."

Thomas said to him, "My Lord and my God!"

Then Jesus told him, "Because you have seen me, you have believed; blessed are those who have not seen and yet have believed."

RECONCILIATION

An act of reconciling, as when former enemies agree to an amicable truce.

RECONCILE

To win over to friendliness; cause to become amicable (to reconcile hostile persons). To compose or settle (a quarrel, dispute, etc.).

> *Therefore if anyone is in Christ, he is a new creature; the old things passed away; behold, new things have come. Now all these things are from God, who reconciled us to Himself through Christ and gave us the ministry of reconciliation, namely, that God was in Christ reconciling the world to Himself, not counting their trespasses against them, and He has committed to us the word of reconciliation. 2 Corinthians 5:17-19*

> *Then Esau ran to meet him and embraced him, and fell on his neck and kissed him, and they wept. Genesis 33:4*

> *"Therefore if you are presenting your offering at the altar, and there remember that your brother has something against you, leave your offering there before the altar and go; first be reconciled to your brother, and then come and present your offering. Matthew 5:23-24*

The Prodigal Son

James Edward

Then He said, "A certain man had two sons. The younger of them [inappropriately] said to his father, 'Father, give me the share of the property that falls to me.' So he divided the estate between them. A few days later, the younger son gathered together everything [that he had] and traveled to a distant country, and there he wasted his fortune in reckless *and* immoral living. *Now when he had spent everything, a severe famine occurred in that country and he began to do without* and *be in need. So he went and forced himself on one of the citizens of that country, who sent him into his fields to feed pigs. He would have gladly eaten the [carob] pods that the pigs were eating [but they could not satisfy his hunger], and no one was giving* anything *to him. But when he [finally] came to his senses, he said, 'How many of my father's hired men have more than enough food, while I am dying here of hunger! I will get up and go to my father, and I will say to him, "Father, I have sinned against heaven and in your sight. I am no longer worthy to be called your son; [just] treat me like one of your hired men."' So he got up and came to his father. But while he was still a long way off, his father saw him and was moved with* compassion *for him, and ran and embraced him and kissed him. And the son said to him, 'Father, I have sinned against heaven and in your sight; I am no longer worthy to be called your son.' But the father said to his servants, 'Quickly bring out the best robe [for the guest of honor] and put it on him; and give him a [b]ring for his hand, and sandals for his feet. And bring the fattened calf and slaughter it, and let us [invite everyone and] feast and celebrate; for this son of mine was [as good as] dead and is alive again; he was lost and has been found.' So they began to celebrate.*

"Now his older son was in the field; and when he returned and approached the house, he heard music and dancing. So he summoned one of the servants and began *asking what this [celebration] meant. And he said to him, 'Your brother has come, and your father has killed the fattened calf because he has received him back safe and sound.' But the elder brother became angry* and *deeply resentful and was not willing to go in; and his father came out and* began *pleading with him. But he said to his father, 'Look! These many years I have served you, and I have never neglected or disobeyed your command. Yet you have never given me [so much as] a young goat, so that I might celebrate with my friends; but when this [other] son of yours arrived, who has devoured your estate with immoral women, you slaughtered that fattened calf for him!' The father said to him, 'Son, you are always with me, and all that is mine is yours. But it was fitting to celebrate and rejoice, for this brother of yours was [as good as] dead and* has begun *to live. He was lost and has been found.'" Luke 15:11-32*

REDEEMED

To recover ownership by paying a specified sum. To pay off, as a promissory note. To turn in and receive something in exchange. To set free; rescue. To save from sin. To make up for: redeemed his earlier mistake.

Christ REDEEMED us from the curse of the law by becoming a curse for us, for it is written: cursed is everyone who is hung on a tree. Galatians 3:13

James Edward

Let the REDEEMED of the Lord say so, who he hath REDEEMED from the hand of the enemy. Psalm 107.2

RELIGION

A specific fundamental set of beliefs and practices generally agreed upon by a number of persons or sects.

Note: Interesting fact...Jesus hated religion. It was always the religious leaders that He came against even at one point telling them they weren't going to Heaven and they were keeping others from going also.[2]

Religion teaches us a series of rules supposedly to get to God, but God never wanted that, He always wanted relationship with man even from the beginning with Adam whom He made to fellowship with. God made Himself a friend.

I heard a minister say once that Jesus never healed the same way twice in the Bible because He knew that men would make it a doctrine and teach that that was the only way to be healed.

Jesus stepped on the scene calling God Father and thereby introducing God's true name to man. He is our Father. Until then no one ever referred to God as Father. As a matter of fact Jesus went further because He said Abba which was basically Daddy! God always desired an intimate friendship/relationship with man and never a series of steps. Can you imagine coming to your earthly father and saying "Dear Father who birthed me and takes

---

[2] *Woe to you, teachers of the law and Pharisees, you hypocrites! You shut the door of the kingdom of heaven in people's faces. You yourselves do not enter, nor will you let those enter who are trying to. Matthew 23:13*

care of me, please feed me tomorrow". That's silly and that is about how silly it is to approach our heavenly Father that way.

> *And we all agree our religion contains amazing revelation: He was revealed in the flesh, vindicated by the Spirit, seen by angels, proclaimed among Gentiles, believed on in the world, taken up in glory. 1 Timothy 3:16*
>
> *If you claim to be religious but don't control your tongue, you are fooling yourself, and your religion is worthless. Religion that is pure and undefiled before God, the Father, is this: to visit orphans and widows in their affliction and to keep oneself unstained from the world. James 1:26-27*
>
> *"But woe to you Pharisees! For you pay tithe of mint and rue and every kind of garden herb, and yet disregard justice and the love of God; but these are the things you should have done without neglecting the others. Luke 11:42*
>
> *For I testify about them that they have a zeal for God, but not in accordance with knowledge. For not knowing about God's righteousness and seeking to establish their own, they did not subject themselves to the righteousness of God. For Christ is the end of the law for righteousness to everyone who believes. Romans 10:2-4*
>
> *When the Pharisee saw it, he was surprised that He had not first ceremonially washed before the meal. But the Lord said to him, "Now you Pharisees clean the outside of the cup and of the platter; but inside of you, you are full of robbery and wickedness. "You foolish ones, did not He who made the outside make the inside also? Luke 11:38-40*

James Edward

RENEW

To be restored to a former state; become new or as if new again.

> *Who satisfies your mouth with good things; so that your youth is renewed like the eagles. Psalm 103:5*
>
> *Create in me a clean heart, O God; and renew a right spirit within me. Psalm 51:10*
>
> *Do not conform to the pattern of this world, but be transformed by the renewing of your mind. Then you will be able to test and approve what God's will is--his good, pleasing and perfect will. Romans 12:2*

RESPECT

Esteem, admiration. Proper acceptance or courtesy. To hold in esteem or honor. Recognition of a person's worth or of a personal quality, trait or ability.

> *Give to everyone what you owe them: If you owe taxes, pay taxes; if revenue, then revenue; if respect, then respect; if honor, then honor. Romans 13:7*
>
> *Rise in the presence of the aged, show respect for the elderly and revere your God. I am the Lord. Leviticus 19:32*

RESPONSIBILITY

The state or fact of being responsible, answerable, or accountable for something within one's power, control, or management.

> *"For we will all stand before the judgment seat of God. So then each of us will give an account of himself to God." Romans 14:10, 12*

> "Whoever conceals his transgressions will not prosper, but he who confesses and forsakes them will obtain mercy." Proverbs 28:13

RIGHTEOUSNESS (right standing)

Characterized by uprightness or morality. Morally right or justifiable. Acting in an upright, moral way/ virtuous. From righteous meaning friends, not enemies.

> *For just as through the disobedience of the one man the many were made sinners, so also through the obedience of the one man the many will be made righteous. Romans 5:17 - 19*

> *He made Him who knew no sin to be sin on our behalf, so that we might become the righteousness of God in Him. 2 Corinthians 5:21*

> *What then shall we say? That the Gentiles, who did not pursue righteousness, have obtained it, a righteousness that is by faith; Romans 9:30*

James Edward

S

SABBATH

The seventh day of the week, Saturday, as the day of rest and religious observance among Jews and some Christians.
From the Hebrew sabat, meaning to stop, to cease, or to keep.

> *"Remember the Sabbath day, to keep it holy. Six days you shall labor, and do all your work, but the seventh day is a Sabbath to the Lord your God. On it you shall not do any work, you, or your son, or your daughter, your male servant, or your female servant, or your livestock, or the sojourner who is within your gates. For in six days the Lord made heaven and earth, the sea, and all that is in them, and rested on the seventh day. Therefore the Lord blessed the Sabbath day and made it holy. Exodus 20:8-11*
>
> *And he said to them, "The Sabbath was made for man, not man for the Sabbath". Mark 2:27*
>
> *For the Son of Man is Lord, even over the Sabbath! Matthew 12:8*

SACRED

Devoted or dedicated to a deity or to some religious purpose; consecrated. Entitled to veneration or religious respect by association with divinity or divine things; holy. Reverently dedicated to some person, purpose, or object.

> *Do not give that which is holy (the sacred thing) to the dogs, and do not throw your pearls before hogs, lest they trample upon them with their feet and turn and tear you in pieces. Matthew 7:6*

> *He who regards the day as sacred, so regards it for the Master's sake; and he who eats certain food eats it for the Master's sake, for he gives thanks to God; and he who refrains from eating it refrains for the Master's sake, and he also gives thanks to God. Romans 14:6*

> *Therefore I tell you, every sin and blasphemy (every evil, abusive, injurious speaking, or indignity against sacred things) can be forgiven men, but blasphemy against the [Holy] Spirit shall not and cannot be forgiven. Matthew 12:31*

> *Blind fools! Which is greater, the gold or the temple that makes the gold sacred? Matthew 23:17*

SACRIFICE

The offering of animal, plant, or human life or of some material possession to a deity, as in propitiation or homage. The person, animal, or thing so offered. The surrender or destruction of something prized or desirable for the sake of something considered as having a higher or more pressing claim.

> *Abraham said, "God will provide for Himself the lamb for the burnt offering, my son." So the two of them walked on together. Genesis 22:8*

James Edward

> *Through Jesus, therefore, let us continually offer to God a sacrifice of praise--the fruit of lips that openly profess his name. Hebrews 13:15*
>
> *Greater love has no one than this: to lay down one's life for one's friends. John 15:13*
>
> *So Christ was sacrificed once to take away the sins of many; and he will appear a second time, not to bear sin, but to bring salvation to those who are waiting for him. Hebrews 9:28*
>
> *To do what is right and just is more acceptable to the Lord than sacrifice. Proverbs 21:3*
>
> *But go and learn what this means: 'I desire mercy, not sacrifice.' For I have not come to call the righteous, but sinners." Matthew 9:13*
>
> *He who did not spare his own Son, but gave him up for us all—how will he not also, along with him, graciously give us all things? Romans 8:32*
>
> *Every priest stands daily ministering and offering time after time the same sacrifices, which can never take away sins; but he, having offered one sacrifice for sins for all time, sat down at the right hand of god, waiting from that time onward until his enemies be made a footstool for his feet. For by one offering he has perfected for all time those who are sanctified. Hebrews 10:11-14*

SAINT

A Christian Believer – The word "saint" comes from the Greek word hagios, which means "consecrated to God, holy, sacred, pious". Reference the writings of Paul where he referred to the Saints at Ephesus, Romans, etc. According to Paul, a saint is someone who is "sanctified in Christ Jesus." This describes all who believe in Christ and are made holy by his grace. Also included in the definition are" all that call upon the name of Jesus Christ
From the Greek hagios meaning the state of being pure in one's relationship to God.

> *But Ananias answered, "Lord, I have heard from many about this man, how much evil he has done to your saints at Jerusalem. Acts 9:13*
>
> *Now as Peter went here and there among them all, he came down also to the saints who lived at Lydda. Acts 9:32*
>
> *And I did so in Jerusalem. I not only locked up many of the saints in prison after receiving authority from the chief priests, but when they were put to death I cast my vote against them. Acts 26:10*
>
> *Greet every saint in Christ Jesus. The brothers who are with me greet you. Philippians 4:21*
>
> *...that you may welcome her in the Lord in a way worthy of the saints, and help her in whatever she may need from you, for she has been a patron of many and of myself as well. Romans 16:*
>
> *...to equip the saints for the work of ministry, for building up the body of Christ, Ephesians 4:12*

James Edward

> *To the church of God that is in Corinth, to those sanctified in Christ Jesus, called to be saints together with all those who in every place call upon the name of our Lord Jesus Christ, both their Lord and ours: 1 Corinthians 1:2*

SALVATION

The act of saving or protecting from harm, risk, loss, etc. The state of being so saved or protected. A source, cause or means of being saved or protected from harm, risk, etc. Deliverance from the power and penalty of sin; redemption.

Note: the word translated into English as Salvation in the Greek is soteria or sozo which mean complete and total deliverance from poverty, sickness and death.
To go deeper in Hebrew Jesus' name is Yeshua which translated means Salvation. Jesus himself is Salvation, complete and total deliverance from poverty, sickness and death.

> *Salvation is found in no one else, for there is no other name under heaven given to men by which we must be saved. Acts 4:12*

> *She will give birth to a Son, and you shall name Him Jesus (The Lord is salvation), for He will save His people from their sins." Matthew 1:21*

> *I am not ashamed of the gospel, for it is the power of God for salvation [from His wrath and punishment] to everyone who believes [in Christ as savior], to the Jew first and also to the Greek. Romans 1:16*

SANCTIFIED

Made holy (set apart for God); consecrated.

Sanctify them through thy truth: thy word is truth. John 17:17

Who gave (yielded) Himself up [to atone] for our sins [and to save and sanctify us], in order to rescue and deliver us from this present wicked age and world order, in accordance with the will and purpose and plan of our God and Father." Galatians 1:4

Wherefore Jesus also, that he might sanctify the people with his own blood, suffered without the gate. Hebrews 13:12

And the very God of peace sanctify you wholly; and I pray God your whole spirit and soul and body be preserved blameless unto the coming of our Lord Jesus Christ. 1 Thessalonians 5:23

For by a single offering he has perfected for all time those who are being sanctified. Hebrews 10:14

SANCTUARY

A sacred or holy place. An especially holy place in a temple or church. Any place of refuge.

Judaism
A. the Biblical tabernacle or the Temple in Jerusalem.
B. the holy of holies of these places of worship.

God is our refuge and strength, A very present help in trouble. Psalm 46:1

Let them construct a sanctuary for Me, that I may dwell among them. Exodus 25:8

James Edward

> *The name of the LORD is a strong tower; the righteous runs into it and is safe. Proverbs 18:10*

SATAN (The Accuser)

The chief evil spirit; the great adversary of humanity; the devil. Adversary, accuser, Prosecuting Attorney. From Greek Satanas, from Hebrew Satan "adversary, one who plots against another," from Satan "to show enmity to, oppose, plot against," one who opposes, obstructs, or acts as an adversary.

> *Then I heard a loud voice in heaven say: "Now have come the salvation and the power and the kingdom of our God, and the authority of his Messiah. For the accuser of our brothers and sisters, who accuses them before our God day and night, has been hurled down. Revelations 12:10*

> *Again there was a day when the sons of God came to present themselves before the LORD, and Satan also came among them to present himself before the LORD. The LORD said to Satan, "Where have you come from?" Then Satan answered the LORD and said, "From roaming about on the earth and walking around on it." The LORD said to Satan, "Have you considered My servant Job? For there is no one like him on the earth, a blameless and upright man fearing God and turning away from evil. And he still holds fast his integrity, although you incited Me against him to ruin him without cause."*
> *Satan answered the LORD and said, "Skin for skin! Yes, all that a man has he will give for his life. "However, put forth Your hand now, and touch his bone and his flesh; he will curse You to Your face." So the LORD said to Satan, "Behold, he is in your power, only spare his life." Job 2:1-6*

And the tempter came and said to Him, "If You are the Son of God, command that these stones become bread." Matthew 4:3

The sting of death is sin, and the power of sin is the law. 1 Corinthians 15:56

SAVIOR

A person who saves, rescues or delivers another person or a thing from danger or harm
Note: Our Savior's name is Yeshua which means – Savior or He who saves. Jesus is taken from the Greek Ioses, but if you were to meet him on the street today and ask what His name is He would say Yeshua.
Also Christ is not his last (surname) name. Christ is His title so He is Jesus the Christ or in Hebrew He would be called Yeshua the Messiah.

"For the Son of Man has come to seek and to save that which was lost." Luke 19:10

...for today in the city of David there has been born for you a Savior, who is Christ the Lord. Luke 2:11

For God so [greatly] loved and dearly prized the world, that He [even] gave His [One and] only begotten Son, so that whoever believes and trusts in Him [as savior] shall not perish, but have eternal life. John 3:16

And we have seen and testify that the Father has sent his Son to be the savior of the world. 1 John 4:14

James Edward

> *But when the kindness of God our savior and His love for mankind appeared, He saved us, not on the basis of deeds which we have done in righteousness, but according to His mercy, by the washing of regeneration and renewing by the Holy Spirit, Titus 4:7*

SEEK

To search for. To endeavor to obtain or reach.

> *For the Son of Man came to seek and to save the lost. Luke 19:10*

> *And so I tell you, keep on asking, and you will receive what you ask for. Keep on seeking, and you will find. Keep on knocking, and the door will be opened to you. Luke 11:19*

> *But seek first his kingdom and his righteousness, and all these things will be given to you as well. Matthew 6:33*

SELFISH

Devoted to or caring only for oneself; concerned primarily with one's own interests, benefits, welfare, etc., regardless of others.

> *Pride goes before destruction, a haughty spirit before a fall. Proverbs 16:18*

> *But he gives us more grace. That is why scripture says: God opposes the proud but gives grace to the humble. James 4:6*

SHIELD

A broad piece of armor, varying widely in form and size, carried apart from the body, usually on the left arm, as a defense against swords, lances, arrows, etc. A person or thing that protects. To hide or conceal; protect by hiding.

> The LORD is my strength and my shield; My heart trusts in Him, and I am helped; Therefore my heart exults, And with my song I shall thank Him. Psalm 28:7
>
> After these things the word of the LORD came to Abram in a vision, saying, "Do not fear, Abram, I am a shield to you; Your reward shall be very great." Genesis 15:1
>
> Our soul waits for the LORD; He is our help and our shield. Psalm 33:20
>
> Every word of God is tested; He is a shield to those who take refuge in Him. Proverbs 30:5
>
> Surely, LORD, you bless the righteous; you surround them with your favor as with a shield. Psalm 5:12

SHEPHERD

A person who herds, tends, and guards sheep. A person who protects, guides, or watches over a person or group of people. A member of the clergy. The Shepherd, Jesus the Christ. To tend or guard as a shepherd. To watch over carefully.
From the Greek poimaino meaning to provide spiritual care, protection and spiritual food for a "flock" of Christians and protect it from spiritual wolves.

> Be on guard for yourselves and for all the flock, among which the Holy Spirit has made you overseers, to shepherd the church of God which He purchased with His own blood. I know that after my departure savage wolves will come in among you, not sparing the flock; and from among your

own selves men will arise, speaking perverse things, to draw away the disciples after them. Acts 20:28-30

The Lord is my shepherd; I shall not want.
He makes me to lie down in green pastures; He leads me beside the still waters.
He restores my soul; He leads me in the paths of righteousness for His name's sake.

Yea, though I walk through the valley of the shadow of death I will fear no evil; for You are with me; Your rod and Your staff, they comfort me.

You prepare a table before me in the presence of my enemies; You anoint my head with oil; my cup runs over. Surely goodness and mercy shall follow me all the days of my life; and I will dwell in the house of the Lord forever. Psalm 23

"I am the good shepherd. The good shepherd lays down his life for the sheep. John 10:11

When Jesus landed and saw a large crowd, he had compassion on them, because they were like sheep without a shepherd. So he began teaching them many things. Mark 6:34

SIGHT

The power or faculty of seeing; perception of objects by use of the eyes; vision.

Now the earth was corrupt in God's sight, and the earth was filled with violence. Genesis 6:11

But Noah found favor in the sight of the Lord. Genesis 6:8

I am giving all this land, as far as you can see, to you and your descendants as a permanent possession. Genesis 13:15

The blind receive their sight and the lame walk, the lepers are cleansed, and the deaf hear, the dead are raised up, and the poor have the gospel preached to them. Matthew 11:5

Then Ananias went to the house and entered it. Placing his hands on Saul, he said, "Brother Saul, the Lord--Jesus, who appeared to you on the road as you were coming here--has sent me so that you may see again and be filled with the Holy Spirit." Acts 9:17

SIN (missing the mark)

Transgression of divine law. Any act regarded as such a transgression, esp. a willful violation of some religious or moral principle.
Note: Most of us have a hard time accepting the fact that we are sinners and I understand why.
If you ask someone are they a sinner MOST times they are going to take offense and say they are not a bad person.

That is where the problem comes in because we don't have a clear understanding of what a sinner is.

Here is a radical statement so sit down and hold onto something and please just hear me out.
Being a Sinner does not make you a bad person nor is Hell a place for JUST bad people.

James Edward

Whew I said it so I hope you're still with me and now I'll explain. In Romans Paul does a great job of distinguishing your do from your who. Being a Sinner (I'm capitalizing the S for distinction) is different from sinning.

Being a Sinner is how you were born (period). You had nothing to do with it no more than you had a say in your nationality, gender, race or eye color. Your parents did that and as such since you came from Adam then Adam's transgression made us all Sinners.

Being a Sinner means you are an enemy to God and the penalty for being a Sinner is death, but once again – had nothing to do with you and the great thing is God did something about that.

Now the act of sinning is different. That is what you do not who you are. So once you are "saved" by accepting what God's Son did then we are done with the issue of you being a Sinner.

From that point forward you are a Saint, but you will still commit sins while you are on this side, but no worries because Jesus took care of that too. (there is a lot more to this, but I'm keeping it simple)

Ok so here is an example I like to use. Imagine you are born on a train and the train is heading for a cliff. So in other words you are born with a ticket to die. What Jesus did was to get you off that particular train so now you aren't headed for sure and immediate death.

However and maybe unfortunately He didn't remove your ability to commit sins. Yes you are saved, but you can still sin however though that is a big deal with God, but maybe not so much because if it really really was then He would have gotten you saved and took you out of this world. He didn't do that so I have to think His plan for leaving us here is a good one.

So then should we as Saints just go willy nilly sinning all the live long day? That's what they asked Paul every time he taught the Gospel and his answer was always GOD FORBID NO!

No we don't take our new found liberty (freedom) and just go sinning because there are consequences for sin and you'll get hurt and God doesn't want you hurt.

I'll put it like my pastor says sin carries its own penalty in it". If you put your hand on a hot stove the stove will punish you and God will still love you, but He doesn't want you burned. If you rob a bank God will still love you, but He'll have to love you in jail because the bank and police are going to ensure you go there.
If you go out and sleep with someone's spouse, God will still love you, but that persons spouse isn't going to and they may want to hurt you and God doesn't want them to hurt you.

See inherent in every sin is Its own punishment and God doesn't want you to be punished so that's why He doesn't want you to sin.

The truth is that being a Sinner and being a good person are not mutually exclusive. You can be a Sinner and still be a good person.

Oh and by the way I said Hell is not just a place for bad people. Remember being born on the train? Well according to the Bible if you don't get off the train you go to Hell and that has nothing to do with you being a good person or not. Very simply the penalty for sin is death so we either accept what God did by offering His son to pay that penalty in our stead or we pay it ourselves.

James Edward

> *When Adam sinned, sin entered the world. Adam's sin brought death, so death spread to everyone, for everyone sinned. Romans 5:12*
>
> *So whoever knows the right thing to do and fails to do it, for him it is sin. James 4:17*
>
> *God made him who had no sin to be sin for us, so that in him we might become the righteousness of God. 2 Corinthians 5:21*
>
> *For the wages of SIN is death, but the gift of God is eternal life in Christ Jesus our Lord. Romans 6:23*

SLANDER

A malicious, false, and defamatory statement or report.

> *And the men, which Moses sent to search the land, who returned, and made all the congregation to murmur against him, by bringing up a slander upon the land. Numbers 14:36*
>
> *You sit and speak against your brother; you slander your own mother's son. Psalm 50:20*
>
> *It is out of the heart that evil thoughts come, as well as murder, adultery, sexual immorality, stealing, false testimony, and slander. Matthew 15:19*
>
> *But Jesus said, "Don't stop him, because no one who works a miracle in my name can slander me soon afterwards." Mark 9:39*

Or can we say as some people slander us by claiming that we say "Let's do evil that good may result"? They deserve to be condemned! Romans 3:8

But now you must also put away all the following: anger, wrath, malice, slander, and filthy language from your mouth. Colossians 3:8

Miriam & Aaron Slander Moses
Then Miriam and Aaron spoke against Moses because of the Ethiopian woman whom he had married; for he had married an Ethiopian woman. So they said, "Has the Lord indeed spoken only through Moses? Has He not spoken through us also?" And the Lord heard it. (Now the man Moses was very humble, more than all men who were on the face of the earth.)

Suddenly the Lord said to Moses, Aaron, and Miriam, "Come out, you three, to the tabernacle of meeting!" So the three came out. Then the Lord came down in the pillar of cloud and stood in the door of the tabernacle, and called Aaron and Miriam. And they both went forward. Then He said,

"Hear now My words: If there is a prophet among you, I, the Lord, make Myself known to him in a vision; I speak to him in a dream.
Not so with My servant Moses; He is faithful in all My house.
I speak with him face to face, even plainly, and not in dark sayings; and he sees the form of the Lord.
Why then were you not afraid to speak against My servant Moses?"

James Edward

So the anger of the Lord was aroused against them, and He departed. And when the cloud departed from above the tabernacle, suddenly Miriam became leprous, as white as snow. Then Aaron turned toward Miriam, and there she was, a leper. So Aaron said to Moses, "Oh, my lord! Please do not lay this sin on us, in which we have done foolishly and in which we have sinned. Please do not let her be as one dead, whose flesh is half consumed when he comes out of his mother's womb!"

So Moses cried out to the Lord, saying, "Please heal her, O God, I pray!"

Then the Lord said to Moses, "If her father had but spit in her face, would she not be shamed seven days? Let her be shut out of the camp seven days and afterward she may be received again." So Miriam was shut out of the camp seven days, and the people did not journey till Miriam was brought in again. And afterward the people moved from Hazeroth and camped in the Wilderness of Paran. Numbers 12

SLAVE

A person who is the property of and wholly subject to another; bond servant. A person entirely under the domination of such influence or person.

So you are no longer a slave, but a son; and since you are a son, God has made you also an heir. Galatians 4:7

For we know that our old self was crucified with him so that the body of sin might be done away with, that we should no longer be slaves to sin – because anyone who has died has been freed from sin. Romans 6:6 & 7

What then? Shall we sin because we are not under the law but under grace? By no means! Don't you know that when you offer yourselves to someone as obedient slaves, you are slaves of the one you obey—whether you are slaves to sin, which leads to death, or to obedience, which leads to righteousness? But thanks be to God that, though you used to be slaves to sin, you have come to obey from your heart the pattern of teaching that has now claimed your allegiance. You have been set free from sin and have become slaves to righteousness.
I am using an example from everyday life because of your human limitations. Just as you used to offer yourselves as slaves to impurity and to ever-increasing wickedness, so now offer yourselves as slaves to righteousness leading to holiness. When you were slaves to sin, you were free from the control of righteousness. What benefit did you reap at that time from the things you are now ashamed of? Those things result in death! But now that you have been set free from sin and have become slaves of God, the benefit you reap leads to holiness, and the result is eternal life. For the wages of sin is death, but the gift of God is eternal life in Christ Jesus our Lord. Romans 6: 15 – 23

SON OF MAN

Jesus Christ, especially at the Last Judgment.

> *...just as the Son of Man did not come to be served, but to serve, and to give His life a ransom for many." Matthew 20:28*

James Edward

Then He said to me, "Son of man, stand on your feet that I may speak with you!" Ezekiel 2:1

"But so that you may know that the Son of Man has authority on earth to forgive sins"--then He said to the paralytic, "Get up, pick up your bed and go home." Matthew 9:6

And He began to teach them that the Son of Man must suffer many things and be rejected by the elders and the chief priests and the scribes, and be killed, and after three days rise again. Mark 8:31

...saying, "The Son of Man must suffer many things and be rejected by the elders and chief priests and scribes, and be killed and be raised up on the third day." Luke 9:22

Jesus said to him, "You have said it yourself; nevertheless I tell you, hereafter you will see the Son of Man sitting at the right hand of power, and coming on the clouds of heaven." Matthew 26:64

What is man that You take thought of him, And the son of man that You care for him? Yet You have made him a little lower than God, And You crown him with glory and majesty! You make him to rule over the works of Your hands; You have put all things under his feet. Psalm 8:4-6

SOUL

Man is a tripartite being just like God because you are made in His image and likeness. Spirit, soul and boy. Another way to say this is that you are a Spirit, you have a soul (mind will and emotions) and you live in a body which is your earth suit. As long as you live here

you have a body and when you lose it (it dies) you have to leave earth. But your spirit, which is the real you still lives.
Spirit from the Greek pneuma which literally means 'that which is breathed or blown.' Then the LORD God formed a man from the dust of the ground and breathed into his nostrils the breath of life, and the man became a living being - Genesis 2:7.
Soul from the Greek psyche meaning sensory-self, soul or life.
Body from the Greek soma meaning body, flesh.

> *Then he said to me: Prophesy to the breath, prophesy, son of man! Say to the breath: Thus says the Lord God: From the four winds come, O breath, and breathe into these slain that they may come to life. I prophesied as he commanded me, and the breath entered them; they came to life and stood on their feet, a vast army. Ezekiel 37:9-10*

Unfortunately the Bible uses Spirit and Soul interchangeably in some places, but look at these next two verses to see that it also clearly distinguishes the three parts of man.

> *Hebrews 4:12, "For the word of God is quick, and powerful, and sharper than any two-edged sword, piercing even to the dividing asunder of soul and spirit, and of the joints and marrow, and is a discerner of the thoughts and intents of the heart."*

> *1 Thessalonians 5:23, "And the very God of peace sanctify you wholly; and I pray God your whole spirit and soul and body be preserved blameless unto the coming of our Lord Jesus Christ."*

James Edward

Note: One significant thing about your earth suit is that to operate in this world you have to have one. Remember God gave Man dominion of this earth and as the late Myles Monroe said He didn't say "let us share dominion with man".
God is sovereign, but He has also subjected Himself to His word[3] and because of that every time God wanted to do something in this realm He went and found Himself a man to do it or command it from Adam to Abraham, Isaac, Jacob, all of the Prophet's, Priests and Kings and even to Jesus Himself.

> *For it is impossible for the blood of bulls and goats to take away sins. Therefore, when he comes into the world, he says, "sacrifice and offering you have not desired, but a body you have prepared for me; in whole burnt offerings and sacrifices for sin you have taken no pleasure. Hebrews 10:4-6*

SOVEREIGN

A monarch; a king, queen, or other supreme ruler. A person who has supreme power or authority. Having supreme rank, power, or authority. Supreme; preeminent; indisputable. Greatest in degree; utmost or extreme. Being above all others in character, importance, excellence, etc.

> *Pride goes before destruction, a haughty spirit before a fall. Proverbs 16:18*

---

[3] *For ever, O LORD, thy word is settled in heaven. Psalm 119:89*
I bow down toward your holy temple and give thanks to your name for your grace and truth; for you have made your word greater than the whole of your reputation. Psalm 138:2(The Complete Jewish Bible)

But he gives us more grace. That is why scripture says: God opposes the proud but gives grace to the humble. James 4:6

SPIRIT

The principle of conscious life; the vital principle in humans, animating the body or mediating between body and soul. The incorporeal part of humans. Conscious, incorporeal being, as opposed to matter.
Note: See also Soul. Man is a tripartite being Spirit, Soul and Body. It is your spirit that is born again when you receive Christ, your mind is renewed daily and you'll get your new body later.

> *And the earth was without form, and void; and darkness was upon the face of the deep. And the Spirit of God moved upon the face of the waters. Genesis 1:1*

> *Then the Lord God formed man from the dust of the ground and breathed into his nostrils the breath or spirit of life, and man became a living being. Genesis 2:7*

> *And they come in unto Noah, unto the ark, two by two of all the flesh in which is a living spirit. Genesis 7:15*

> *And Ishmael lived 137 years; then his spirit left him, and he died and was gathered to his kindred. Genesis 25:17*

> *God is spirit, and his worshipers must worship in the Spirit and in truth. John 4:24*

STEALING

To take (the property of another or others) without permission or right, esp. secretly or by force.

James Edward

> *He who has been stealing must steal no longer, but must work, doing something useful with his own hands, that he may have something to share with those in need. Ephesians 4:68*
>
> *The thief comes only to steal and kill and destroy; I have come that they may have life, and have it to the full. John 10:10*
>
> *Let him who stole steal no longer, but rather let him labor, working with his hands what is good, that he may have something to give him who has need. Ephesians 4:28*

STRENGTH

The quality or state of being strong; physical power; vigor.

> *For the foolishness of God is wiser than man's wisdom and the weakness of God is stronger than man's strength. 1 Corinthians 1:25*
>
> *I can do all this through him who gives me strength. Philippians 4:13*
>
> *But they that wait upon the LORD shall renew their strength; they shall mount up with wings as eagles; they shall run, and not be weary; and they shall walk, and not faint. Isaiah 40:31*

SUCCESS

The favorable or prosperous termination of attempts or endeavors. The attainment of wealth, position, honors or the like.

Keep this Book of the Law always on your lips; meditate on it day and night, so that you may be careful to do everything written in it. Then you will be prosperous and successful. Joshua 1:8

The LORD was with Joseph, so he succeeded in everything he did as he served in the home of his Egyptian master. Genesis 39:2

James Edward

T

TAX COLLECTOR (Publican)

Freelance tax collectors who worked for the Romans. Often Jews. A person who collected public taxes. Any collector of taxes, tolls, tribute, or the like.

Note: The Jews were very good at hiding their money from the Romans so the Romans would hire Jews to collect from Jews assuming that they would know the tricks their fellow countrymen would use.

The Romans would designate an amount that they wanted and anything the tax collector received above that amount was theirs to keep and the Roman Army would back the tax collector in receiving that amount. Example – Rome wants ten percent, but the Tax Collector demands thirty or fifty percent from the citizen and there is nothing you can do about it.

This is why tax collectors we considered extortionist and traitors to their people.

> *For if you love those who love you, what reward do you have? Do not even the tax collectors do the same? Matthew 5:46*
>
> *Then it happened that as Jesus was reclining at the table in the house, behold, many tax collectors and sinners came and were dining with Jesus and His disciples. Matthew 9:10*
>
> *The Pharisee stood and was praying this to himself: 'God, I thank You that I am not like other people: swindlers, unjust, adulterers, or even like this tax collector. Luke 18:11*

THANKSGIVING

The act of giving thanks; grateful acknowledgment of benefits or favors, especially to God.

> *Enter his gates with thanksgiving and his courts with praise; give thanks to him and praise his name. Psalm 100:4*

> *Give thanks to the LORD, for he is good; his love endures forever. Psalm 107:1*

> *For this reason, ever since I heard about your faith in the Lord Jesus and your love for all God's people I have not stopped giving thanks for you, remembering you in my prayers. Ephesians 1:15-16*

> *For everything God created is good, and nothing is to be rejected if it is received with thanksgiving, because it is consecrated by the word of God and prayer. 1 Timothy 4:4-5*

> *...do not be anxious about anything, but in everything by prayer and supplication with thanksgiving let your requests be made known to God. Philippians 4:6*

TITHE

Sometimes tithes. the tenth part of agricultural produce or personal income set apart as an offering to God or for works of mercy, or the same amount regarded as an obligation or tax for the support of the church, priesthood, or the like.

Note: The purpose of the tithe was first as an obligation to the Lord since everything was His you basically were redeeming (buying) back the right to use the ninety percent and thereby also

James Edward

receiving a blessing for your obedience. Tithing is honoring God and a form of worship.

> And he blessed him and said, "Blessed be Abram by God Most High, possessor of heaven and earth; and blessed be God Most High, who has delivered your enemies into your hand!"
> And Abram gave him a tenth of everything. *Gen. 14:19–20*
>
> *"Will a person rob God? Yet you are robbing me! But you ask, "How are we robbing you?' "By the tithe and the offering. Malachi 3:8*
>
> *"Bring the whole tithe into the storehouse, that there may be food in my house. Test me in this," says the Lord Almighty, "and see if I will not throw open the floodgates of heaven and pour out so much blessing that there will not be room enough to store it." Malachi 3:10*
>
> *And all the tithe of the land, whether of the seed of the land, or of the fruit of the tree, is the LORD'S: it is holy unto the LORD. Leviticus 27:30*
>
> *Woe unto you, scribes and Pharisees, hypocrites! For ye pay tithe of mint and anise and cumin, and have omitted the weightier matters of the law, judgment, mercy, and faith: these ought ye to have done, and not to leave the other undone. Matthew 23:23*

TRANSFORM

To change in form, appearance, or structure; metamorphose. To change in condition, nature or character, convert. To change into another Substance, transmute. To radically change the outward form or inner character: a frog transformed into a prince.

> Do not conform any longer to the pattern of this world, but be transformed by the renewing of your mind. Then you will be able to test and approve what God's will is – His good, pleasing and perfect will. Romans 12:2

> But our citizenship is in heaven, and from it we await a Savior, the Lord Jesus Christ, who will transform our lowly body to be like his glorious body, by the power that enables him even to subject all things to himself. Philippians 3:20-21

> After six days Jesus took Peter, James, and John and led them up on a high mountain by themselves to be alone. He was transformed in front of them. Mark 9:2

> And we all, with unveiled face, continually seeing as in a mirror the glory of the Lord, are progressively being transformed into His image from [one degree of] glory to [even more] glory, which comes from the Lord, [who is] the Spirit. 2 Corinthians 3:18

TRINITY
Also called Blessed Trinity, Holy Trinity. The union of three persons (Father, Son, and Holy Ghost) in one Godhead, or the threefold personality of the one Divine Being.
Note: See also Elohim as in Genesis 1:1 "In the beginning, God created the heavens and the earth." The word God here is translated from the Hebrew Elohim which is plural so a more accurate translation would read "In the beginning the God's created the heavens and the earth."

James Edward

Therefore go and make disciples of all nations, baptizing them in the name of the Father and of the Son and of the Holy Spirit, Matthew 28:19

May the grace of the Lord Jesus Christ, and the love of God, and the fellowship of the Holy Spirit be with you all. 2 Corinthians 13:14

The LORD said, "Behold, they are one people, and they all have the same language. And this is what they began to do, and now nothing which they purpose to do will be impossible for them. "Come, let Us go down and there confuse their language, so that they will not understand one another's speech." Genesis 11:6-7

And the LORD God said, "The man has now become like one of us, knowing good and evil. He must not be allowed to reach out his hand and take also from the tree of life and eat, and live forever." Genesis 3:22

Then God said, "Let Us make man in Our image, according to Our likeness; and let them rule over the fish of the sea and over the birds of the sky and over the cattle and over all the earth, and over every creeping thing that creeps on the earth." God created man in His own image, in the image of God He created him; male and female He created them. Genesis 1:26-27

TRUTH

The true or actual state of a matter. Conformity with or reality; verity. A verified or indisputable fact, proposition, principle or the like. The state or character of being true.
From the Greek aletheia which describes either physical truth that

can be verified by the five senses or spiritual truth which factual information which is not perceptible through the five senses, but can only be discerned by a non-physical part of a human called the "spirit."

Then you will know the truth and the truth will set you free. John 8:32

> *Jesus answered, I am the way and the truth and the life. No one comes to the Father except through me. John 14:6*
>
> *"But the hour is coming, and is now here, when the true worshipers will worship the Father in spirit and truth, for the Father is seeking such people to worship him." John 4:23*
>
> *"Jesus said to him, "I am the way, and the truth, and the life. No one comes to the Father except through me." John 14:6*
>
> *"Stand therefore, having fastened on the belt of truth, and having put on the breastplate of righteousness..." Ephesians 6:14*

TRUST

Firm reliance; confident belief; faith. Reliance on something in the future; hope. To rely or depend on. Have confidence in. To be confident; hope. To expect with assurance; assume. To believe. From the Greek pistis meaning "belief" or "faith."

> *By faith Abraham, when called to go to a place he would later receive as his inheritance, obeyed and went, even though he did not know where he was going By faith he*

James Edward

made his home in the promised land like a stranger in a foreign country; he lived in tents, as did Isaac and Jacob, who were heirs with him of the same promise. For he was looking forward to the city with foundations, whose architect and builder is God. Hebrews 11:8

Trust in the Lord with all your heart and lean not on your own understanding; in all your ways acknowledge him and he will make your paths straight. Proverbs 3:5 & 6

For the Scripture says, "Whoever believes in Him [whoever adheres to, trusts in, and relies on Him] will not be disappointed [in his expectations]." Romans 10:11

"The LORD is my rock, and my fortress, and my deliverer; my God, my strength, in whom I will trust; my buckler, and the horn of my salvation, and my high tower." *Psalm 18:2*

"I will say of the LORD, He is my refuge and my fortress: my God; in him will I trust." *Psalm 91:2*

James Edward

V

VISION

The act or power of anticipating that which will or may come to be. As opposed to sight (seeing things as they are) vision is seeing things as they can be.

> *Where there is no vision, the people are unrestrained, but happy is he who keeps the law. Proverbs 29:18*

> *After these things the word of the LORD came unto Abram in a vision, saying, Fear not, Abram: I am thy shield, and thy exceeding great reward. Genesis 15:1*

> *That night the Lord came to him in a vision, and said, I am the God of your father Abraham: have no fear for I am with you, blessing you, and your seed will be increased because of my servant Abraham. Genesis 26:24*

> *Now go, write this vision before them on a tablet and note it in a book that it may remain unto the last day, forever, unto all ages. Isaiah 30:8*

> *And the LORD answered me, and said, write the vision, and make it plain upon tables, that he may run that reads it. For the vision is yet for an appointed time, but at the end it shall speak, and not lie: though it tarry, wait for it; because it will surely come, it will not tarry. Habakkuk 2:2-3*

James Edward

W

WEALTH

A great quantity or store of money, property or other riches. Plentiful amount, abundance.

> *But remember the LORD your God, for it is he who gives you the ability to produce wealth, and so confirms his covenant, which he swore to your ancestors, as it is today. Deuteronomy 8:18*

> *The Lord has greatly blessed my master [Abraham], and he has become great (wealthy, powerful); He has given him flocks and herds, and silver and gold, and servants and maids, and camels and donkeys. Genesis 24:35*

> *And the man [Isaac] became great and gained more and more until he became very wealthy and extremely distinguished; Genesis 26:13*

WISDOM

The quality or state of being wise; sagacity, discernment or insight.

WISE (the ability to apply knowledge)
Having the power of discerning and judging properly as to what is true or right; possessing discernment, judgment or discretion.

> *Yet we do speak wisdom among those who are mature; a wisdom, however, not of this age nor of the rulers of this age, who are passing away; but we speak God's wisdom in*

a mystery, the hidden wisdom which God predestined before the ages to our glory; the wisdom which none of the rulers of this age has understood; for if they had understood it they would not have crucified the Lord of glory; 1 Corinthians 2:6 – 8

"The fear of the LORD is the beginning of wisdom: and the knowledge of the holy is understanding." Proverbs 9:10

But of him are ye in Christ Jesus, who of God is made unto us wisdom, and righteousness, and sanctification, and redemption: 1 Corinthians 1:30

Solomon's wisdom surpassed the wisdom of all the sons of the east and all the wisdom of Egypt. For he was wiser than all men, than Ethan the Ezrahite, Heman, Calcol and Darda, the sons of Mahol; and his fame was known in all the surrounding nations. He also spoke 3,000 proverbs, and his songs were 1,005. 1 Kings 4:30-32

Let no one deceive himself. If anyone among you thinks that he is wise in this age, let him become a fool that he may become wise. 1 Corinthians 3:18

Walk with the wise and become wise; associate with fools and get in trouble. Proverbs 13:20

WITCHCRAFT

The art or practices of a witch; sorcery; magic. Magical influence; witchery.

"There shall not be found among you anyone who makes his son or his daughter pass through the fire, one who uses

James Edward

> *divination, one who practices witchcraft, or one who interprets omens, or a sorcerer. Deuteronomy 18:10*
>
> *I will render your witchcraft powerless, and mediums will no longer exist among you. Micah 5:12*
>
> *And they repented not of their murders, nor of their witchcrafts, nor of their fornication, nor of their thefts. Revelations 9:21*
>
> *God was doing extraordinary and unusual miracles by the hands of Paul, so that even handkerchiefs or face-towels or aprons that had touched his skin were brought to the sick, and their diseases left them and the evil spirits came out [of them]. Then some of the traveling Jewish exorcists also attempted to call the name of the Lord Jesus over those who had evil spirits, saying, "I implore you and solemnly command you by the Jesus whom Paul preaches!" Seven sons of one [named] Sceva, a Jewish chief priest, were doing this. But the evil spirit retorted, "I know and recognize and acknowledge Jesus, and I know about Paul, but as for you, who are you?" Then the man, in whom was the evil spirit, leaped on them and subdued all of them and overpowered them, so that they ran out of that house [in terror, stripped] naked and wounded. This became known to all who lived in Ephesus, both Jews and Greeks. And fear fell upon them all, and the name of the Lord Jesus was magnified and exalted. Acts 19:11-17*

WITNESS

To see, hear or know by personal presence and perception.
Note: from the Greek martur meaning a person who can testify as

to what he has seen, heard or otherwise experienced. The English word "martyr" means a person who dies for trusting in God or Jesus, or for a "cause." But this differs greatly from the Greek meaning of martur, "a witness."

> ...came to me, and standing near said to me, 'Brother Saul, receive your sight!' And at that very time I looked up at him. "And he said, 'The God of our fathers has appointed you to know His will and to see the Righteous One and to hear an utterance from His mouth. 'For you will be a witness for Him to all men of what you have seen and heard. Acts 22:14-15

> But you will receive power when the Holy Spirit comes on you; and you will be my witnesses in Jerusalem, and in all Judea and Samaria and to the ends of the earth. Acts 1:8

> Therefore, since we are surrounded by so great a cloud of witnesses, let us also lay aside every weight, and sin which clings so closely, and let us run with endurance the race that is set before us, Hebrews 12:1

WORLD

The earth or globe, considered as a planet. From the Greek kosmos meaning the inhabitants of the earth, men, the human family the ungodly multitude; the whole mass of men alienated from God, and therefore hostile to the cause of Christ world affairs, the aggregate of things earthly. The whole circle of earthly goods, endowments riches, advantages, pleasures, etc.

> "For God so loved the world, that He gave His only begotten Son, that whoever believes in Him shall not

perish, but have eternal life." For God did not send the Son into the world to judge the world, but that the world might be saved through Him. John 3:16

For the promise to Abraham or to his descendants that he would be heir of the world was not through the Law, but through the righteousness of faith. Romans 4:13

The next day he saw Jesus coming to him and said, "Behold, the Lamb of God who takes away the sin of the world! John 1:29

WORD OF GOD

Often we use this term to refer to the Bible, but that is not necessarily true.
The Greeks used two words to refer to the word.

Rhema which referred to the written word of God meaning something spoken.

Logos which is a title that refers to Jesus the Christ Himself.

Logos specifically translates to the expression of a thought so in John 1:1 where we read "In the beginning was the Word. And the Word was with God and the Word was God. He was in the beginning with God." This is specifically referring to Jesus. However in Hebrews 6:5 where we have and have tasted the goodness of the word of God and the powers of the age to come. This word is rhema meaning the something spoken.

Logos

Sanctify them in the truth; your word is truth. John 17:17

for it is made holy by the word of God and prayer. 1 Timothy 4:5

For the word of God is living and active, sharper than any two-edged sword, piercing to the division of soul and of spirit, of joints and of marrow, and discerning the thoughts and intentions of the heart. Hebrews 4:12

And we also thank God constantly for this, that when you received the word of God, which you heard from us, you accepted it not as the word of men but as what it really is, the word of God, which is at work in you believers. 1 Thessalonians 2:13

You search the Scriptures because you think that in them you have eternal life; and it is they that bear witness about me, John 5:39

Rhema

and have tasted the goodness of the word of God and the powers of the age to come, Hebrews 6:5

But he answered, "It is written,

" 'Man shall not live by bread alone,

but by every word that comes from the mouth of God.' " Matthew 4:4

and take the helmet of salvation, and the sword of the Spirit, which is the word of God, Ephesians 6:17

Note: One more thing worthy of mention is that not every word in the Bible is the Word of God. A good way to look at this is that the Bible is

James Edward

like a Court Stenographer who's job is to sit there and type everything that is spoken in court for the purpose of recording the trial.

Well the Bible can be looked at the same such so that it records what was spoken, but that doesn't make mean what was spoken came from God. Some examples are in Psalm 90:10 Moses said *"Our days may come to seventy years, or eighty, if our strength endures; yet the best of them are but trouble and sorrow, for they quickly pass, and we fly away."*
This is not the word of God because God said in *Genesis 6:3 "My Spirit shall not strive with man forever, because he also is flesh; nevertheless his days shall be one hundred and twenty years."*
Again both were recorded by the stenographer so to speak, but only one can be classified as the word of God.
Also in Job 1:21 Job said *"Naked I came from my mother's womb, and naked I will depart. The LORD gave and the LORD has taken away; may the name of the LORD be praised."*
If you know this story you know God didn't take anything from Job the Devil did, but Job didn't know that so he said God did it.

God said in for God's gifts and his call are irrevocable. Romans 11:29 and in *James 1:17 Every good and perfect gift is from above, coming down from the Father of the heavenly lights, who does not change like shifting shadows.*
Lastly (for now) in 1 Corinthians 7:8 Paul makes it clear he is speaking when he says *"Now to the unmarried and the widows I say: It is good for them to stay unmarried, as I do."* Which is a direct contradiction to the word God spoke in Genesis 9:7 *"be fruitful and multiply"*.

This is why it is important for us to rightly divide the word.

WORSHIP

Reverent honor and homage paid to God or a sacred personage, or to any object regarded as sacred. To feel an adoring reverence or regard for (any person or thing).
Note: In the Old Testament for worship is the Hebrew word "shachah" which means "to bow down, to depress, to prostrate

oneself". In the New Testament, the Geek word "proskyneo" is used and this means to "kiss the hand towards the one, in token of reverence".

> "But the hour is coming, and now is, when the true worshippers shall worship the Father in spirit and in truth: for the Father seeks such to worship him." John 4:23

> "Through him then let us continually offer up a sacrifice of praise to God, that is, the fruit of lips that acknowledge his name." Hebrews 13:15

> "Oh come, let us worship and bow down; let us kneel before the Lord, our Maker!" Psalm 95:6

James Edward

BASIC TENETS (BELIEFS) OF CHRISTIANITY

A belief or principle held by a group as being true.

In one God, who exists in three Persons—the Father, Son and Holy Spirit. He is loving, holy and just.

That the Bible is God's Word. It is inspired and accurate. It is our perfect guide in all matters of life.

That sin has separated us all from God, and that only through Jesus Christ can we be reconciled to God.

That Jesus Christ is both God and Man. He was conceived by the Holy Spirit and born of the virgin Mary. He led a sinless life, took all our sins upon Himself, died and rose again. Today, He is seated at the right hand of the Father as our High Priest and Mediator.

That salvation is the gift of God to man. This gift is effected by grace through faith in Jesus Christ and it results in works pleasing to God.

That water baptism is a symbol of the cleansing power of God and a testimony of our faith in the Lord Jesus Christ.

That the Holy Spirit is our Comforter. He guides us in all areas of our lives. He also blesses us with spiritual gifts and empowers us to yield the fruit of the Spirit.

That the Holy Communion is a celebration of Jesus' death and our remembrance of Him.

James Edward

That God wants to transform, heal and provide for us, so that we can live blessed and victorious lives that will impact and help others.

That we are called to preach the gospel to all nations.

That our Lord Jesus Christ is coming back again just as He promised.

APOSTLES CREED

A creed, dating back to about a.d. 400, traditionally ascribed to Christ's apostles and having widespread acceptance in the Christian church. The apostles' creed is a good summary of Christian doctrine.

> *I believe in God, the Father Almighty,*
> *the Creator of heaven and earth,*
> *and in Jesus Christ, His only Son, our Lord:*
> *Who was conceived of the Holy Spirit,*
> *born of the Virgin Mary, suffered under Pontius Pilate, was crucified, died, and was buried.*
> *He descended into hell.*
> *The third day He arose again from the dead.*
> *He ascended into heaven and sits at the right hand of God the Father Almighty, whence He shall come to judge the living and the dead.*
> *I believe in the Holy Spirit, the holy catholic [4]church, the communion of saints, the forgiveness of sins, the resurrection of the body,*
> *and life everlasting.*
> *Amen.*

---

[4] Holy catholic church in this case does not mean the Roman Catholic Church, but the Universal Church or all bodies of Christian believers. Catholic means universal.

James Edward

WHY DO I NEED TO BE SAVED

... for all have sinned and fall short of the glory of God, Romans 3:23

Behold, I was brought forth in iniquity, and in sin did my mother conceive me. Psalm 51:5

Surely there is not a righteous man on earth who does good and never sins. Ecclesiastes 7:20

HOW CAN I BE SAVED

For the wages of sin is death, but the free gift of God is eternal life in Christ Jesus our Lord. Romans 6:23

Then he brought them out and said, "Sirs, what must I do to be saved? And they said, "Believe in the Lord Jesus, and you will be saved, you and your household." Acts 16:30-31

But what does it say? "the word is near you, in your mouth and in your heart"-- that is, the word of faith which we are preaching, that if you confess with your mouth Jesus as Lord, and believe in your heart that God raised Him from the dead, you will be saved; for with the heart a person believes, resulting in righteousness, and with the mouth he confesses, resulting in salvation. Romans 10:8-10

OUR NEW COVENANT

This is the covenant I will establish with the people of Israel
after that time, declares the Lord.
I will put my laws in their minds
and write them on their hearts.
I will be their God,
and they will be my people.
No longer will they teach their neighbor,
or say to one another, 'Know the Lord,'
because they will all know me,
from the least of them to the greatest.
For I will forgive their wickedness
and will remember their sins no more."

Hebrews 8:10-12

BIBLIOGRAPHY

Holy Bible: containing the Old and New Testaments; NKJV, New King James Version, 1991

Zondervan NIV Study Bible. Fully rev. ed. Kenneth L. Barker, gen. ed. Grand Rapids: Zondervan, 2002.

The English Standard Version Bible: Containing the Old and New Testaments with Apocrypha. Oxford: Oxford UP, 2009

New International Version. [Colorado Springs]: Biblica, 2011 BibleGateway.com. Web. 3 Mar. 2011.

"Bible Hub: Search, Read, Study the Bible in Many Languages." Bible Hub: Search, Read, Study the Bible in Many Languages. N.p., n.d. Web. 21 Feb. 2016.

"Bible Questions Answered by GotQuestions.org." GotQuestions.org. N.p., n.d. Web. 23 Feb. 2016.

"BibleGateway." .com: A Searchable Online Bible in over 150 Versions and 50 Languages. N.p., n.d. Web. 21 Feb. 2016.

"Old & New Testament." Online Bible. N.p., n.d. Web. 21 Feb. 2016.

Dictionary.com. Dictionary.com, n.d. Web. 21 Feb. 2016.

"Studies of New Testament Words." Studies of New Testament Words. N.p., n.d. Web. 21 Feb. 2016.

"OpenBible.info." OpenBible.info. N.p., n.d. Web. 21 Feb. 2016.

"Hebrew for Christians." Hebrew for Christians - Learn Hebrew for FREE! N.p., n.d. Web. 21 Feb. 2016.

INDEX

A
Abundant, 21
Abundantly, 21
Acknowledge, 21
Acknowledges, 21
Adam, 22
Adultery, 23
Adversary, 52, 139
Advocate, 42
Aletheia, 161
Almost too good to be true news, 70
Angels, 23, 73, 102, 130
Angels, 23
Anoint, 24
Anointed, 25, 33, 35, 71, 119
Apostle, 25
Ask, 25
Assembly, 39, 40
Authority, 26

B
Baptism, 27
Baptizo, 27
Believe, 27, 28
Bible, 28, 42, 113, 124, 152
Bible, 28
Bishop, 29
Bless, 31
Blessed, 31
Breastplate, 162

C
Captive, 33
Care, 33
Careful, 33, 34
Cares, 33, 34
Charis, 62
Cheating, 35
Cheerful, 34
Christ, 21, 22, 25, 27, 28, 34, 35, 36, 37, 38, 45, 54, 62, 63, 67, 69, 71, 72, 73, 76, 84, 87, 91, 92, 95, 100, 101, 104, 107, 108, 109, 115, 121, 124, 126, 128, 130, 135, 136, 137, 138, 140, 142, 147, 150, 152, 154, 160, 161, 168, 170
Christ, 35
Comfort, 36
Comforter, 36
Compassion, 37
Condemn, 38
Condemnation, 38
Condemned, 38
Confess, 38
Confidence, 27, 40, 71, 77, 162
Confidence, 40
Conform, 39, 160
Conformed, 40, 101
Congregation, 39
Consecrate, 41
Convocation, 40
Convoking, 40
Counsel, 41
Counselor, 41, 42
Covenant, 42, 43, 63, 88, 101, 167
Covenant, 42

James Edward

Create, 43
Creator, 43
Cristos, 35
Cult, 44
Curse, 44, 45
Cursed, 45
D
Daimonion, 47
Deny, 48
Desire, 48
Devil, 23, 102, 139
Didasko, 117
Do give me what i don't deserve, 72
Dominion, 48
Don't give me what i do deserve, 100
Doubt, 49
E
Earnest, 51
Earnestly, 51
Elohim, 51
Enemies, 52, 53
Enemy, 52
Enslaved, 33
Envy, 53
Episkopos, 29
Eternal, 53, 54
Eternal life, 53
Eternity, 54
Euangelion, 117
Evangelist, 54
Evil, 55
Exousia, 26
F
Fair, 57

Faith, 27, 28, 38, 50, 67, 77, 85, 90, 104, 107, 113, 119, 121, 132, 158, 159, 162, 171
Fallen from grace, 61
Father, 21, 26, 27, 35, 36, 37, 39, 42, 48, 51, 52, 53, 61, 65, 79, 92, 107, 108, 116, 127, 130, 138, 140, 160, 161, 162, 174
Father, 61
Favor, 72
Favor, 62
Fear, 62
Fellowship, 63
Fool, 64
Forgive, 64, 65
Fornication, 64
Forsaken, 65
Free, 65, 66
G
Generous, 67
Gentile, 67
Gentle, 68
Glad, 68
Glory, 68
God, 69, 84, 92
Godhead, 79, 160
Good, 70
Gospel, 70, 71
Gossip, 71
Grace, 72
Greed, 73
Guilty, 72
H
Hagah, 99

Hagios, 136
Happy, 75
Heal, 75
Health, 75
Heathen, 67
Heir, 76
Help, 76
Helper, 42, 79
High priest, 77
Holiday, 77
Holy, 78, 79
Holy day, 77
Holy spirit, 26, 27, 36, 42, 51, 52, 64, 79, 92, 141, 144, 161, 170
Homologeo, 38
Homosexual, 79, 80
Homosexuality, 80
Honest, 80
I
Image, 83
Iniquity, 83
Invisible, 84
Ioses, 140
J
Jealous, 87, 88
Jealousy, 87
Jesus appears to thomas, 125
Jesus christ, 23, 136, 137
Jew, 88
Joy, 34, 62, 68, 88, 92
Joy, 88, 89
Judaism, 77, 88, 93, 123, 138
Justice, 89
Justification, 89

Justified, 89
Justify, 89, 90
K
Kind, 91
King, 91
Kosmos, 170
L
Law, 93
Lie, 97
Likeness, 94
Logos, 171
Lord, 1, 21, 22, 25, 31, 33, 34, 36, 37, 39, 42, 43, 50, 52, 55, 57, 61, 62, 63, 65, 68, 71, 77, 78, 79, 83, 89, 91, 94, 95, 97, 101, 105, 111, 113, 114, 115, 119, 120, 125, 126, 129, 130, 131, 133, 135, 136, 137, 138, 140, 143, 144, 147, 148, 149, 150, 152, 154, 158, 159, 160, 161, 163, 165, 167, 168, 174
Lord, 31, 41, 44, 48, 52, 69, 70, 76, 83, 88, 89, 91, 95, 100, 104, 115, 118, 120, 139, 142, 152, 155, 156, 158, 159, 161, 163, 165, 167, 168
Lord of lords, 91
Lost, 95, 96
Love, 96
Lying, 97
M
Makarios, 31
Martur, 169
Meditate, 99
Meek, 99
Melchizedek, 77, 118

James Edward

Mercy, 72
Mercy, 100
Messiah, 35
Mind, 100
Minister, 101
Ministers, 42
Miriam, 148, 149
Missing the mark, 144
Money, 104
Moses, 22, 44, 73, 83, 89, 93, 100, 147, 148, 149
Mother, 105
Mutter, 99

N

Need, 107
Never, 65, 108
New, 108, 109

O

Ordained, 111
Overseer, 29, 30

P

Pagan, 67
Patience, 113
Peace, 113
Pharisees, 130, 159
Pistis, 162
Pneuma, 152
Potential, 114
Poverty, 114, 115
Praise, 115
Pray, 116
Prayed, 116
Prayer, 116
Praying, 116

Pride, 117, 121, 141, 153
Priest, 118
Promise, 119
Prophet, 119
Prosecuting attorney, 139
Prosperity, 120
Prosperous, 120
Prostestant, 121
Protect, 120
Protestant, 25, 54
Proud, 121, 141, 154
Provide, 121
Psyche, 152

R

Rabbi, 123
Reality, 123
Reconcile, 126
Reconciliation, 126
Redeemed, 128, 129
Religion, 129
Religious, 31, 39, 44, 77, 78, 101, 118, 123, 130, 133, 144
Renew, 131
Respect, 131
Responsibility, 131
Rhema, 171, 172
Right standing, 62, 132
Righteousness, 132

S

Sabbath, 41, 70, 77, 78, 133
Sabbath, 133
Sacred, 133
Sacrifice, 134
Saint, 136

Lord Make It Plain | So I Can Understand - Definitions

Salvation, 137
Sanctified, 137
Sanctify, 138
Sanctuary, 138
Satan, 139
Savior, 137, 140, 141
Seek, 141
Selfish, 141
Set apart for god, 78, 137
Shalom, 113, 114
Shepherd, 142
Shield, 141
Sight, 143
Sin, 144, 147
Sinned, 147
Slander, 147
Slave, 149
Soma, 152
Son of man, 96, 133, 140, 141, 150, 151
Son of man, 150
Soteria, 137
Soul, 151
Sovereign, 48, 91, 125, 153
Sovereign, 153
Sozo, 137
Spirit, 25, 33, 42, 48, 52, 71, 72, 79, 83, 88, 89, 93, 94, 101, 130, 134, 151, 152, 154
Spirit, 79, 154
Steal, 155
Stealing, 154, 155
Strength, 155

Success, 155
Synagogue, 123
T
Talking with god, 116
Teacher, 123
Tempter, 140
Tenth part, 158
Thanksgiving, 158
The ability to apply knowledge, 167
The accuser, 139
The prodigal son, 126
Tithe, 158
Tithes, 158
Transform, 159
Transformed, 39, 160
Trinity, 160
Tripartite, 151, 154
Trust, 162, 163
Truth, 161, 162
U
Unorthodox, 44
V
Vision, 165
W
Wealth, 167
Wisdom, 167
Wise, 167, 168
Witchcraft, 168
Witness, 97, 169
World, 170
Worship, 173
Y
Yeshua, 137, 140

James Edward

NOTES

NOTES

NOTES

NOTES

Made in the USA
Charleston, SC
22 March 2016